GREEK SCRIPTS

An illustrated introduction

GREEK SCRIPTS
An illustrated introduction

edited by

PAT EASTERLING

and

CAROL HANDLEY

SOCIETY FOR THE PROMOTION
OF
HELLENIC STUDIES

2001

© 2001 Society for the Promotion of Hellenic Studies

ISBN 0–902984–17–9

CONTENTS

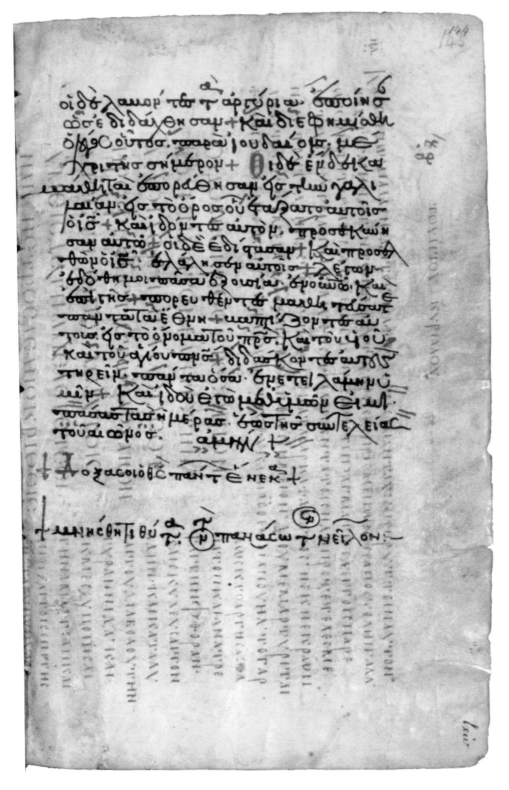

The 'Codex Zacynthius', a palimpsest:
Gospels with marginal commentary, eighth-ninth century (lower script);
Gospel lectionary, thirteenth century (upper script).
(see Chapter 6, fig. **12**)

PREFACE

This book has an unusual history. It owes its origin to a discussion among friends and colleagues in the Classical Faculty of the University of Cambridge, prompted by Eric Handley with a different end in view, which was to find ways of marking the centenary in 1998 of the first publication of Oxyrhynchus Papyri. One of the ideas that was mooted then was that we should produce a slim picture-book illustrating the range of scripts used for Greek texts of various kinds, from the time when Greek was first written down until the development of printing. Greek scripts are typically dealt with by different specialists—epigraphers, papyrologists, numismatists, palaeographers—but a volume that would bring together a selection of material in an accessible way might, we thought, be useful and appealing to anyone with an interest in Greek, and provide a stimulus to further reading and exploration.

The idea, originally Carol Handley's, was taken up with generous enthusiasm by the volunteers whose contributions make up this volume. It began as a modest and quite informal collection intended for amateur production and relatively local circulation. Meanwhile, the Society for the Promotion of Hellenic Studies had recently decided to broaden the scope of the occasional publications they undertake in addition to the annual *Journal of Hellenic Studies* and *Archaeological Reports*. They wanted, in particular, to publish work of interest to a wider readership than that of the traditional scholarly monograph, and so when the design (by Eric Handley) and content of *Greek Scripts* became known to the Editorial Committee of the Society, the present form was agreed. We are grateful to the Society, and we thank Lyn Rodley for her expert involvement in the production of this collaborative enterprise.

P. E. E.
C. M. H.

CAMBRIDGE
January 2001

1 The earliest writers of Greek
JOHN KILLEN

As far as we know, Greek was the first European language to be recorded in written form. Mycenaean Greek, an extremely archaic form of the language most closely related to the dialects spoken in Arcadia and Cyprus in later times, is found on the clay tablets written in the Linear B syllabic script which have been discovered in six Bronze Age palaces in Crete and on the Greek mainland. The tablets from the mainland palaces of Pylos, Mycenae, Thebes and Tiryns and from Khania in Crete date from the thirteenth century BC; and those from Knossos in Crete may actually have been written in the fourteenth century (or even in some cases in the late fifteenth). The next oldest Greek inscription is the Classical Cypriot script, a relative of Linear B. This consists of the single word *o-pe-le-ta-u*, the genitive of a man's name and presumably an indication of the ownership of the object, found incised on a metal spit from Palaipaphos in Cyprus dated by its excavators to the eleventh century. The earliest Greek inscriptions in alphabetic script date from the middle of the eighth century BC.

Linear B, deciphered in 1952 by Michael Ventris, is undoubtedly an adaptation, for the purposes of writing Greek, of the earlier Cretan Linear A script. We are not certain when and where the adaptation took place. Some scholars feel that the development of complex society on the Greek mainland is such that writing is likely to have been needed there as early as the sixteenth century. Others believe that Linear B was not evolved until after 1450, after the Greeks arrived in Crete.

1 An inscribed transport jar found at Thebes. The painted inscription includes the place-name *wa-to*, also found on the Knossos tablets, and referring to a place in the west of Crete, which analysis of the clay has shown is the provenance of the jar.

The evidence we have indicates that Linear B was used entirely for bureaucratic purposes: as an aid to the administration of the non-money, non-market redistributive economies of the kingdoms in whose centres the tablets were found. There are no literary works, no legal codes, no diplomatic documents and no public inscriptions. Linear A (still undeciphered) was used to inscribe stone and metal objects with what may be religious dedications; but there is nothing like that in Linear B. Painted Linear B inscriptions are found on a large number of transport jars and other clay vessels found in both Crete and the mainland (fig. **1**); but these inscriptions were very likely only for local bureaucratic purposes, for the administration in the area in which the objects were produced. Though some of the inscribed vessels found on the mainland were produced locally, others are known to have been made in Crete: many in the far west of the island, but others in the central region.

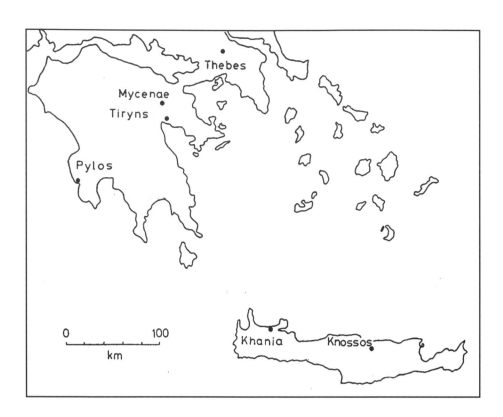

2   The Aegean region, showing the six sites at which Linear B tablets have been discovered.

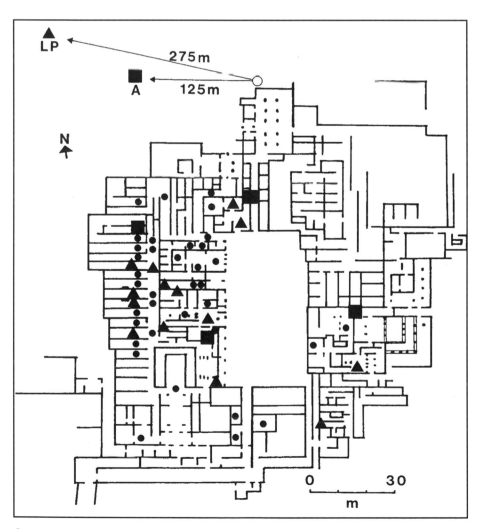

3   A plan of the palace at Knossos, showing the location of the deposits of tablets. [From *AJA* 89 (1985) p. 232]

Size of deposit
(number of tablets)

■   91–500

▲   10–90

●   less than 10

4 The largest of all surviving Linear B tablets, As 1516 at Knossos, the work of scribe 101. It lists men in various groupings, probably assembled for the purposes of work. Here and in fig. **5** the photographs are of casts in the Museum of Classical Archaeology, Cambridge.

Apart from the **jar inscriptions**, the documents written in Linear B are of several types. The great bulk of the inscriptions are on clay **tablets**. These vary in size from slips not more than 2.5 cm long, 1 cm high and 0.4 cm thick to large records with many lines of writing. The largest tablet of all, from Knossos (fig. **4**) is 16 cm wide, 27 cm high, and 2.8 cm thick. The largest archives are at Knossos (3,000+ documents) and Pylos (*ca.* 1,200).

In addition to the tablets, we have **labels**, **sealings** and a few other documents whose purpose is still unclear. All are of clay. Labels were used to indicate the contents of baskets of completed tablets; and sealings were small three-sided nodules of clay with marks inside which show that they were originally moulded round a knot in a piece of string. It has quite recently become clear, from the contents of a cache of these documents found at Thebes in 1982, that the purpose of sealings was to convey information from the outlying parts of the kingdoms to the administrative centres in the palaces. A sealing from Knossos is shown in fig. **7**. At Mycenae, a group of sealings giving details of vessels was found near to a tablet listing vessels of the same type: there is little doubt that this is an example of what must have been a standard practice of converting into tablet form the information brought to the palace on sealings.

5 Tablet Co 903 from Knossos by scribe 107. It records male and female sheep, goats, pigs and oxen, and begins with the west Cretan place-name *wa-to,* also attested on the inscribed transport jar shown in fig. **1**.

The writing on the tablets and other documents consists of three distinct elements: syllabic signs used in groups to form words (which are separated by gaps or by dividers); commodity signs ('ideograms'), some of them more or less pictorial, others syllabic signs used as abbreviations; and, thirdly, signs for measures and numbers. The syllabary (as used by one of the most prolific scribes at Knossos) is shown in fig. **8**; a selection of ideograms is shown in fig. **9**. The signs were normally incised on the document when the clay was still damp; but we have a few examples of additions (such as check marks, indicating the correctness of a calculation) being made later. There are many cases of correction: the original text was deleted either by smearing with the fingers or with the blunt end of the stylus, and a revised text written over it. Some of the tablets are palimpsests: that is, they were originally used to write a different inscription, which has now been expunged. Pointed ivory implements found at Tiryns have been identified as styluses—though E.L. Bennett, the leading expert on Pylian epigraphy, thinks that the tablets there may have been written with thorns inserted in some kind of holder.

When the tablets were written they were first left to dry (probably not in the sun, as has sometimes been suggested) and then stored in wickerwork baskets or wooden boxes. The labels mentioned above have marks on their backs which show that they were pressed against wickerwork when they were still wet; and Sir Arthur Evans found small hinges from boxes among the tablets that he excavated at Knossos. In some palaces at least, tablets were stored on upper floors in plastered rooms above the storage areas. At Knossos, tablets were widely distributed throughout the palace (fig. **3**); at Pylos, however, while there are some small deposits in individual workshops and storage areas, the great majority of

6 Pylos Tablet Cn 1287 (a goat record), *verso.*

It seems plain that there were occasional longueurs in the life of Bronze Age administrative offices. There are a number of tablets that have writings on their backs: among these inscriptions on the *verso* is this drawing of a labyrinth, clearly a doodle.

7   The sealing Ws 1701 from Knossos (scale 5 : 1). As sealings regularly do, it shows a Linear B ideogram on one face, surcharged on a seal impression. The commodity indicated by the ideogram in this instance cannot be identified; the seal impression pictures a bull. The seal impression evidently served to guarantee the authenticity of the ideogram, which could not have been altered without damaging the seal-mark.

the records were found in a special two-room archive complex immediately adjoining the main entrance to the palace. One of these rooms has a low clay bench round its walls; and it is clear that it was on this (and no doubt on some shelves above) that baskets of documents were filed.

At each site, at least the bulk of the tablets we possess date from a single year only: the last year of the activity of the palace in question before its destruction. There are many internal indications that the tablets were only temporary records, not meant to be retained beyond the current year of accounting. The only dates mentioned are of months, never of years (contrast the regular references to regnal years in the cuneiform records from the ancient Near East); and there are frequent descriptions of transactions, products, and so on as *this year's* and *last year's*—descriptions that would have required more specification if the records were intended to be consulted for more than a year. It is clear that none of these lightly dried, temporary records would have been preserved if they had not happened to be baked hard by the fires that consumed the palaces in which they were stored.

It is often wondered whether the Linear B archives originally contained what their writers (ironically) considered to be more permanent records, written on materials like parchment or papyrus. There seems to be evidence for something like this in the Linear A period, in the form of small clay 'envelopes' with marks on the inside showing that they once held something folded. Very few such

Sign	Value	Freq.	Sign	Value	Freq.	Sign	Value	Freq.	Sign	Value	Freq.	Sign	Value	Freq.	Sign	Value	Freq.
	01 DA	1.38		16 QA	0.64		31 SA	1.10		46 JE	0.44		61 O	2.69		76 RA₂	0.25
	02 RO	3.54		17 ZA	0.25		32 QO	0.90		47	0.04		62 PTE	0.09		77 KA	2.33
	03 PA	1.61		18	0.01		33 RA₃	0.07		48 NWA	0.08		63	0.01		78 QE	1.15
	04 TE	3.06		19	0.01		34	0.04		49	0.02		64	0.03		79	0.02
	05 TO	3.08		20 ZO	0.41		35	0.07		50 PU	0.50		65	0.09		80 MA	1.38
	06 NA	1.56		21 QI	0.34		36 JO	4.34		51 DU	0.41		66 TA₂	0.06		81 KU	1.01
	07 DI	0.76		22	0.04		37 TI	1.73		52 NO	2.11		67 KI	1.34		82	0.06
	08 A	3.84		23 MU	0.17		38 E	3.25		53 RI	2.47		68 RO₂	0.14		83	0.06
	09 SE	0.66		24 NE	1.31		39 PI	1.88		54 WA	1.85		69 TU	0.72		(84)	
	10 U	2.64		25 A₂	0.49		40 WI	1.33		55 NU	0.48		70 KO	2.68		85 AU	0.12
	11 PO	1.59		26 RU	0.97		41 SI	1.67		56	0.19		71 DWE	0.02		86	0.02
	12 SO	1.11		27 RE	2.70		42 WO	2.52		57 JA	3.96		72 PE	1.40		87	0.01
	13 ME	1.54		28 I	1.79		43 A₃	0.35		58 SU	0.34		73 MI	0.79		(88)	
	14 DO	0.81		29 PU₂	0.25		44 KE	2.57		59 TA	3.58		74 ZE	0.23		(89)	
	15 MO	0.78		30 NI	1.04		45 DE	1.17		60 RA	3.30		75 WE	2.30		90 DWO	0.02

8 The Linear B syllabary, as written by scribe 117, the major writer of sheep records at Knossos. Each sign is accompanied by its conventional number and sound-value (where known) and a note of its frequency.

No.		No.		No.		No.	
100	VIR	130	OLE	230	HAS	201	VAS
102	MUL	131	VIN	231	SAG	202	VAS
106	OVIS	159	TELA	233	PUG	204	VAS
108	SUS	162	TUN	240	CUR	218	VAS
120	GRA	166		200	VAS	221	VAS

9 A selection of Linear B ideograms, together with their conventional numbers and (Latin) transcriptions. The ideograms in the top line denote (from left to right) a man, olive oil, a spear and a tripod vessel.

Here are drawings of Knossos tablets by two different writers, illustrating the wide differences in scribal hand that can occur:

10 The flax record Nc 4473, the work of scribe 133; all surviving tablets by scribe 133 were found in the Arsenal, 125 m north-west of the palace.

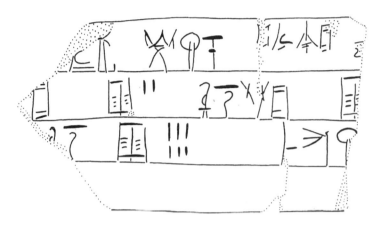

11 The cloth record Le 642, by the elegant writer scribe 103, the author of many of the records of Knossos dealing with wool and textiles and (given that he wrote totalling tablets) perhaps the most senior official in the 'cloth' department of the palace bureaucracy. All scribe 103's output was filed in the area of the Western Magazines.

'envelopes' survive in the Linear B archives, however; and most (if not all) of the business of a Mycenaean kingdom could surely have been done by using Linear B tablets alone. One group of taxation records at Pylos seems to give evidence for what looks like a standard official practice: updating records as the year went on, and carrying forward debts to assessment records for the following taxation year. In this way, Mycenaean officials could have avoided a need for records on any other material.

How much can we say about the scribes who wrote the Linear B documents —the earliest known writers of Greek? The following seems clear or probable:

(a) We can be certain that they were not merely writers of tablets, but palace administrators who were capable of writing. It has been calculated that one scribe writing full time could have written all the tablets we possess in about a fortnight: but at least forty-one different scribal hands, and perhaps as many as seventy, can be identified at Knossos alone. See figs. **10–11**.

(b) Although there are a few generalist scribes who dealt with a number of different administrative topics, the great majority were specialists who concentrated their attention on one or at most two or three aspects of the kingdom's economy. At Knossos, for instance, the scribe to whom J.-P. Olivier has given the number 117 wrote no fewer than 800 tablets dealing with sheep, and (as far as we know) nothing besides these (figs. **12** and **13**). Moreover, when we can establish the find-spots of tablets, these show that all the records written by a particular scribe on a particular subject tended to be filed together, in a single area of the palace. (All scribe no. 117's sheep tablets, for instance, were evidently filed in the Domestic Quarter in the east of the palace.)

12 The fragmentary Knossos sheep record Dv 8836, now in the Liverpool University Archaeological Museum (scale 1.8 : 1). It is by scribe 117, and records a flock of 78 male sheep and 20+ females. The signs at the left (]*no-to*) are part of a place-name *qa-na-no-to* attested in full on other records in this series.

13 The fragmentary Knossos tablet (Dd) 8151, now in University College London (1.8 : 1). It joins with Dd 1374, a sheep tablet in the Heraklion Museum, Crete, and is again by scribe 117, the author of the great majority of flock records at Knossos. It shows the word *ma-ta-u-ro*, the name of the shepherd or owner of the sheep listed.

(c) It looks as if scribes may have learnt their skills *via* an apprenticeship system. Again at Knossos, there are several cases of two scribes working on the same subject having closely similar handwritings; and this is most easily explained on the assumption that one is the master and the other the pupil, or that both are pupils of the same master. (Among the cases in point are two writers of the sheep tablets: scribe 117 has a closely similar hand to scribe 119, who records the wool output of some of the same animals as are recorded in detail on flock records written by scribe 117.)

(d) We can now be certain that, though the scribes were officials who wrote tablets, they themselves did not normally make the documents. A recent study of the fingerprints on the tablets at Knossos has shown that the people who made the blank tablets on which the scribes wrote were normally not the scribes themselves (whose fingerprints are also visible), but either children aged 8–12 or mature adults, the roughness of whose hands suggests that they had earlier had some other occupation (such as rowing or wood-cutting).

(e) Some scribes were peripatetic. As we have seen earlier, it is now clear that sealings were written outside the palaces and then sent into the centres. And not only do we have no evidence for literacy outside the centres, other than the sealings, which immediately suggests that the latter are the work of peripatetic palace officials: one of the sealings at Knossos can certainly be identified as being in the same scribal hand as many of the tablets in the palace archive which are concerned with recording wool and textiles.

We cannot be certain of the names of any of the scribes, at any of the sites from which we have Linear B records: none of the tablets is signed, and no one is described on the tablets as being a scribe. It is just possible, however, that the most prolific scribe at Pylos (no. 1, in Bennett's classification) was called *A-ko-so-ta* (Alxoitās, *vel sim.*). A number of tablets at Pylos refer to a prominent palace official called *A-ko-so-ta*, who is mentioned on one record as performing a tour of inspection outside the palace. Since we know (a) that scribes were officials; (b) that scribes were peripatetic; and (c) that most of the references to *A-ko-so-ta* occur on tablets by scribe 1, who to judge by the extent and importance of his output was clearly a very significant official, it is just conceivable that in speaking in the third person of the activities of *A-ko-so-ta* ('Thus A. received'; 'Thus A. saw'), scribe no. 1 is in fact speaking of his own activities.

SOME FURTHER READING

General

J. Chadwick, *Linear B and Related Scripts* (London 1987)

J. Chadwick, *The Mycenaean World* (Cambridge 1976), especially Ch.2:
'The documentary evidence'

The Mycenaean economy

J.T. Killen, 'The Linear B tablets and the Mycenaean economy', in A. Morpurgo Davies and Y. Duhoux, eds, *Linear B: A 1984 Survey* (Louvain-la-Neuve 1985) 241-305

Linear B scribes and their assistants

J.-P. Olivier, *Les Scribes de Cnossos* (Rome 1967)

T.G. Palaima, *The Scribes of Pylos* (Rome 1988)

K.-E. Sjöquist and P. Åström, *Knossos: Keepers and Kneaders* (Göteborg 1991)

ACKNOWLEDGEMENTS

I am most grateful to the following for permission to reproduce illustrations: Dr J. Bennet and the *American Journal of Archaeology* (3), Professor L. Godart (10–11), Dr C. Mee (12), Professor J.L. Melena (6,7), Dr J.-P. Olivier (2,8,9), Mr G. Owens (13).

The late Dr John Chadwick kindly read a draft of this article before his death in November 1998, and suggested several amendments. I dedicate it to his memory.

2 *The Greek of inscriptions*
JOYCE REYNOLDS

A. DEVELOPING AN ALPHABET

Writing with an alphabet is something that Greek merchants are plausibly supposed to have learnt from Phoenicians early in the eighth century BC. That was after a period when the syllabic script was forgotten in most of Greece. The Phoenician alphabet needed adaptations and supplements to fit the Greek language, since Phoenician had no signs for vowels and a number of superfluous ones for consonants, especially for sibilants. In different areas the necessary modifications were made differently, so that for several centuries there was a confusing variety of usage in the Greek world.

Alphabets might look much the same at first glance in all cities, but fig. **1** shows some significant differences. In Corinth, for instance, a sign like *beta* was used for *epsilon* and a quite different sign for *beta*; in the Euboean alphabet which Greek colonists in Italy passed to the Romans (and hence to us) an (approximately) C-shaped sign—and not Γ—stood for *gamma*; also interesting historically are the variant forms shown for *delta* and *lamda*, which were to develop into D and L. During the second half of the fifth century BC the alphabet of the East Ionians began to gain wider currency, presumably because it represented spoken Greek

Phoenician		Ionian	Athenian	Euboean	Corinthian			
𐤀	'alef	A A	A A	A Λ	A A	Αα	alpha	a
𐤁	bet	B	B	B	⑨	Ββ	beta	b
𐤂	gimel	Γ	Λ	C C	C C	Φγ	gamma	g
𐤃	dalet	Δ	Δ	D Δ	Δ	Δδ	delta	d
𐤄	he	FE	FE	FE	B	Εε	epsilon	e
𐤅	waw	—	F	F	R	F	digamma	w
𐤆	zayin	I	I	I	I	Ζζ	zeta	z
𐤇	het	B H	B H	B H	B H	Ηη	eta	ê
𐤈	tet	⊗⊕⊙	⊗⊕⊙	⊗⊕⊙	⊗⊕⊙	Θθ	theta	th
𐤉	yod	I	I	I	ζ	Ιι	iota	i
𐤊	kaf	K	K	K	ζK	Κκ	kappa	k
𐤋	lamed	ΓΛ	Ľ	Ľ	ΓΛ	Λλ	lamda	l
𐤌	mem	M M	M M	M M M	M M	Μμ	mu	m
𐤍	nun	N N	N N	N N	N N	Νν	nu	n
𐤎	samek	Ŧ	(xs)	X	Ŧ	Ξξ	xi	x
𐤏	'ayin	O	O	O	O	Οο	omicron	o
𐤐	pe'	Γ	Γ	Γ Γ	Γ	Ππ	pi	p
𐤑	sade	—	—	M(?)	M	ϡ	san	s
𐤒	qof	Ϙ	Ϙ	Ϙ	Ϙ	ϙ	koppa	q
𐤓	res	P D	P R	P	P R	Ρρ	rho	r
𐤔	sin	Σ	S	S	—	Σσς	sigma	s
𐤕	taw	T	T	T	T	Ττ	tau	t
		V Y	Y Y V	Y Y V	Y Y V	Υυ	upsiolon	u
		Φ	φ Φ	φ Φ	φ Φ	Φφ	phi	ph
		X	X	Y V	X	Χχ	chi	ch
		Ψ V	(φs)	(φs)	Y V	Ψψ	psi	ps
		Ω Ω	—	—	—	Ωω	omega	ô

1 A table of some early alphabets. [drawn by Sara Owen]

2 A fragment of a tombstone (? late seventh century) lettered in the local alphabet of Cyrene, no doubt brought by the first colonists *ca.* 630 BC.

Γ = *iota*; $\cap$ = *pi*); written *boustrophedon*; sets of three dots separate words or mark the end of groups of words. The stone (limestone) is soft and easily cut, so that the letters (designed freehand) are reasonably well shaped and aligned.

[Photograph and drawing by C. Dobias-Lalou: C. Dobias-Lalou and F.A. Mohamed, *Libya Antiqua* n.s. 1 (1995) 55–60]

rather more accurately than the others—it had signs for long as well as short *e* and *o* and substituted the more precise ει for *e* in εἰμί, for instance. In the year 403/2 BC it was formally adopted as the official Athenian alphabet, and within a quite short time it had superseded all other alphabets for all Greeks.

In the meantime Greeks had been steadily simplifying the somewhat complex Phoenician signs into more symmetrical ones and had also reacted against the Phoenician practice of writing from right to left; they experimented both with left to right and/or with a combination of the two: left to right in one line and right to left in the next (they called it *boustrophedon*, the way that furrows are made by ploughing oxen). In the course of the fifth century BC the left to right direction ousted the others almost entirely.

The first Greeks to learn letters did so, surely, for convenience in their private business transactions; and private use of them, handwritten in pen and ink on papyrus, or with some kind of stylus on a soft material such as wax or lead, or scratched or painted on pots, will have begun the process, although we can hardly doubt that they were soon used for basic records in the newly develop-ing cities of Greece. Within a short time, it seems clear, both private and public users were developing the concept of writing for display.

Some more examples of early alphabets are given in Chapter 3, Section A.

Greeks displayed texts in public places (which were then called inscriptions) much more commonly than we do, not having our alternative means for putting information in front of the public. Since Phoenicians had done this earlier, it is a practice that may have come along with the use of letters itself; but, if so, Greeks very much extended it.

The earliest Greek inscriptions known at present are thought to be of the third quarter of the eighth century BC. They were all privately commissioned, and many intended for use in a domestic context. From the seventh century onwards our record begins to include public ones too (texts of laws, treaties, etc.), and these appear sporadically but increasingly often, with a great outburst in the fifth century, which made them a characteristic feature of Greek civic life. For the fifth-century democracy of Athens it became a matter of principle to make a considerable range of the documents of government accessible to all citizens by inscribing them. The idea caught on and spread—not only in other democracies but also in oligarchies, although in oligarchies the range of what was displayed was narrower. It is not clear how big a readership was ever expected: literacy was always limited, and some inscriptions were so located that to read them was to risk a severe crick in the neck. The illiterate who wished could, no doubt, get someone else to read them aloud; and some public documents available in inscribed form were also read aloud by public heralds in theatres at major civic festivals annually.

If an inscription was ephemeral in content a whitened board or a stretch of plastered wall would provide a surface on which to write with charcoal or paint. Some, however, were meant to last for long periods, even eternity, and often out-of-doors; so that a hard-wearing material was wanted and lettering that would not fade in sunlight nor wash away in rain. We tend to think of inscriptions as typically cut on stone, but that is because stone has a much higher survival rate than other materials used. Wood, for instance, eventually rots, and metals can be profitably melted down for re-use, but stone inscriptions are certainly over-represented in our museums, and, inevitably, provide most of the illustrations shown here. It is necessary to remember that many, perhaps most, of the cut letters were over-painted, probably in red.

3 Bronze plaque with the text of a treaty, late sixth century BC, local script of Elis:
digamma in use, as in ϜPATPA 'treaty', line 1;
ψ = *chi*;
gamma and *delta* as (e.g.) in the Euboean alphabet, fig. **1**, but angled, not rounded.

[Photograph of a cast. *SEG* XI. 1182]

13

In the earliest surviving inscriptions the letters look roughly like those that would be produced with a pen; a little bigger, no doubt, and not linked up as they would be by a running hand, but each dumped down one after the other, without any ado. Over subsequent centuries there was a slow evolution of lettering styles and layouts specifically for display, designed and executed for legibility and to please at the same time. Progress varied from city to city and, no doubt, from mason to mason, but the best workmen were making clear advances in the sixth century and there was something of a breakthrough in the fifth century.

The bronze plaque illustrated in fig. **3** gives the text of a treaty between Elis and Heraea made in the late sixth century BC. It is written from left to right in the local alphabet of Elis; the lettering is designed as freehand, quite neat and well aligned, although the lines tilt upwards towards their ends—as is liable to happen if one pens a text without guide-lines.

In fifth-century Athens in particular the new demand for public inscriptions in large numbers, facilitated by the availability of fine marble nearby and a sufficient public income to meet the bill, led the masons to develop the *stoichedon* (row-by-row) style. For this they laid out a grid on the face of the stone and placed one letter approximately in the centre of each square. In this way any reasonably skilled workman could produce, with relative speed and ease, letters which were neatly shaped and placed in an orderly relation to each other, aligned both vertically and horizontally, so that a reader could keep his place.

Enlargement of
two columns

4   Stone stele (a free-standing block, four-sided) inscribed with an Athenian public decree of 336 BC laying down penalties for attempts to subvert the democracy. It is in the Ionic alphabet and laid out in the *stoichedon* style; monotony is avoided by variations in the placing of the letters within the allotted space, as well as in their heights and shapes. Note the trend towards serifs and the reduction in size of some of the round letters. [From a cast. B.D. Meritt, *Hesperia* 21 (1952) 355–9]

14

By this time, it seems, good masons drew out the text on the stone before they cut it, perhaps using rulers and compasses (compass points are sometimes visible at the centres of circles) although often operating freehand; and the results are efficient, sometimes actually beautiful. But the *stoichedon* style also had a potential for rigidity, and its mechanical allocation of the same number of letters to each line, however oddly that divided words which ran over from one line to the next, shows pattern predominating over meaning in an unintelligent way. In the later fourth century the style was falling out of fashion; the vertical alignment was gradually abandoned for freer spacing and more sensible divisions between words, while more fluid letter-shapes began to appear with serifs at the ends of strokes, presumably imitating the effects of using ink or paint.

5　A damaged marble base for a relief representing the Celtic tribe of the Trumpilini, one of a series at Aphrodisias in Turkey, showing peoples defeated by the Roman emperor Augustus. It illustrates nicely the practice of drawing out a text on the stone before cutting it—in this case with a preliminary scratching which the mason did not overcut precisely. It will not have mattered, since the base was set very high on a façade and the observer at ground level is unlikely to have noticed. [*SEG* XXXI. 929]

6　A marble plaque made for attachment to a wall or the base of a statue, inscribed with a dedication to several Greek gods. It was set up at Koptos in Egypt by Apollonius, agent to King Ptolemy II of Egypt in the first to second quarter of the third century BC. The lettering is finely designed with a ruler and compass; each letter is nicely balanced, and most strokes finished with serifs. The layout unobtrusively emphasises the dedicator's name and title. [A. Bernand, *Les Portes du Desert* (Paris 1984) no. 47]

7   A marble base for a statue of Germanicus Caesar, adoptive son of the Emperor Tiberius, inscribed in rather mannered lettering of about the middle of the first century AD at Aphrodisias in Turkey. The lettering is designed with ruler and compass (compass points are visible in the circles), carefully aligned but not monotonously even in height; shading is another device which helps to create a sense of spontaneity. The layout stresses the final word (and thereby the significance of the honorand) as heir to the imperial throne. The Aphrodisian masons did not develop further the style of serif shown here—if they had, it could easily have led to over-elaboration and illegibility. [*SEG* XXX. 1252]

In the Hellenistic and Roman periods the number of Greek cities in the Middle East grew greatly. For each one, displaying inscriptions was part of the Greek civic tradition, and they followed it as far as materials and finances allowed. Of course in the new political conditions there were some changes of practice. Messages from kings and honours paid to them; honours to the Roman Senate, Roman provincial officials, Roman emperors—these became significant items to be put on display. Then again, as cities became more dependent on financial help from rich citizens, they thought that inscribing the records of their gratitude would stimulate further generosity; and the benefactors themselves wanted to put their names on record, notably on buildings for which they were responsible. We find an increasing number of statue-bases on which cities recorded the virtues of these people at ever greater length, and a growing number of architectural features inscribed on behalf of donors. At the same time, persons below the wealthy class increasingly wanted to inscribe, on their dedications to the gods, their property and their tombs, statements displaying their identities in the manner long before introduced by the rich. Their inscriptions were usually of moderate to poor quality, but perhaps not without some influence on the better ones.

8   A block from a marble architrave in a portico at Aphrodisias, inscribed probably early in the second century AD. In the first line the Roman emperor is honoured, in the second comes the name and rank of the man who paid for this section of the architrave. The style of lettering is one which came into fashion in the city for public inscriptions in the late first century AD and lasted, with minor changes, into the fourth. The letters, designed with ruler and compasses, are basically 'four-square', with incisions finely cut and polished, shading, and strong but not obtrusive serifs; legibility and balance are their hall-marks. [*SEG* XXX. 1255]

9 A marble altar at Aphrodisias, with an ordinary man's dedication to an unnamed god, probably Asclepius, with a prayer for his wife's health.

The altar is passable work, but the inscription is not. Its letters are uneven in height and depth, poorly aligned; probably based on a handwritten draft, with lunate *epsilon* and *sigma*; and *alpha,* perhaps also *mu,* in a form developed for a running-hand. [Unpublished]

In this context we can see a development towards the construction of as many letters as possible with straight strokes, set firmly on a base line (which may be faintly visible), of even height and to some extent of even width—what a Roman might have called a *littera quadrata;* and certainly, some Roman influence can be detected here. At the same time, increasing care was given to the incised lines; a triangular profile with polished sides became normal for the incisions (it catches the light better than a plain incision), often with shading: i.e. variation in the width of the incisions in order to emphasise particular strokes (no doubt imitating the effect of penning or painting).

Letter-sizes now seem more carefully related to the space available and letter-depths to the sizes, effecting greater legibility. Letters might be drawn together or spread out, and words so placed as to highlight particular points. Word divisions are still not nearly as frequent as we should find convenient, but there are more stops and spaces to help the reader than there were. The best examples have a beauty and dignity that is impressive; but there was a certain risk of monotony. Talented masons avoided this by small variations, achieved (for instance) by occasional taller letters, minor variations of spacing, punctuation marks.

Some masons even introduced letter-forms developed for writing with a pen. These appear in less good inscriptions when, we suppose, a careless or incompetent workman copied slavishly onto stone the letter-forms in a draft text written out with a pen: see fig. **9**. By the second century AD (in some places perhaps even earlier) they might be used to give variety in good work—rounded shapes like ∈, ⊂ and ω (called lunate because of the crescent-shaped *sigma*: see fig. **10**),

10 A fragment from a marble stele on which the city of Cyrene had inscribed a series of letters sent to it by emperors in the middle second century AD.

It shows part of an invocation of Good Fortune at the top, part of the title of the Roman Emperor Hadrian in ll. 2–4, of his greeting to the city in l. 5 and of the text of his communication in ll. 6–7. For everything below the heading the mason has used a well-designed alphabet imitated from a book-hand which was meant to recall the look of the actual document. The comparatively small size of the letters made it possible to pack a lot of words into a small space without more loss of legibility than would face the reader of the original. [SEG xxx.1566]

11 A section of a wall in the theatre of Aphrodisias inscribed with documents conferring or confirming the city's privileges. The lettering is clear, decorated, but not to excess, with variations such as an occasional tall letter, spaces etc., which prevent monotony. It also shows erasures of the reference to Aphrodite in the city's name made by Christians, probably in the seventh century AD when that name had been changed to Stauropolis. Erasure from inscriptions of what was no longer politically correct is a regular feature of inscriptions in the Roman period. It is sometimes clear that the erased area was filled by painted words or decorations, so that the scar-like effect was avoided in antiquity.
[J. Reynolds, *Aphrodisias and Rome* (London 1982) 33–43]

oval variants of the same letters (see fig. **15**); squared forms (*sigma* in fig. **13**); pointed ones, with ϵ, Θ and ϲ in a diamond shape; and occasionally there will be found a shape typical of handwriting like the *alpha* of fig. **9**.

These devices were sometimes used with real subtlety, to evoke the appearance of a document as it came from the imperial chancery, for instance, or that of a literary roll when the text introduced passages of verse, as quite frequently happened on tombstones; or, in the late empire, in the texts that detailed the amazing virtues of prominent men.

12 Public notices—warnings, advertisements, etc.—survive less often than the types so far illustrated; but here, from the entrance to the Hadrianic Baths at Aphrodisias, is a warning that anyone with money in his belt or loincloth who fails to show it at the desk will have only himself to blame for its loss. The lettering is clear and pleasing, but businesslike. [Th. Reinach, *Revue des Études Grecques* 19 (1906) 103–5]

13 Here is another notice of the early second century AD from a library in Athens. It announces that no book will be removed, since readers have taken an oath; and that opening times will be from the first to the sixth hours. The lettering is clear but not very elegant; note the squared form of *sigma*. [T.L. Shear, *Hesperia* 5 (1936) 41–2]

14 Apart from public notices, there are also doodles due to people with time on their hands and pointed implements about their persons. This image of a gladiator, labelled as a Thracian (a specific type of gladiator), was scratched on a theatre seat at Aphrodisias, no doubt by a fan waiting for the next fight. [C.M. Roueché, *Performers and Partisans at Aphrodisias* (London 1993) 110]

15 Remains of a text painted on wall-plaster at Aphrodisias recording acclamations for an emperor and his wife, probably in the later fifth century AD. [C.M. Roueché, *Aphrodisias in Late Antiquity* (London 1989) 98–102]

In late Antiquity and the Byzantine period the number of cut stone inscriptions fell off very markedly; it is possible that instead there were more painted inscriptions, like fig. 15, or mosaic ones, such as fig. 16, which are often found in the floors of churches and other public buildings. In the cut stone texts rounded letter-forms were generally now preferred; and there is much experiment in elaborate ornamentation. By the Middle Byzantine period the principal aim seems to have been pattern rather than legibility.

16 Remains of a text in mosaic on the floor of a public building at Aphrodisias, with a record of public works undertaken by a governor in the second half of the fourth century AD. [Sheila Campbell, *The Mosaics of Aphrodisias in Caria* (Toronto 1991) 28–9]

17 A capital from a church built in the fifth–sixth centuries AD at Aphrodisias. The message of the monogram may have been easily understood by a limited number of informed persons (it perhaps conveys the donor's name), but the pattern might give pleasure to many. [C.M. Roueché, *Aphrodisias in Late Antiquity* (London 1989) 161–2]

SOME FURTHER READING

B.F. Cook, *Greek Inscriptions* (London 1987) with many illustrations

M. Guarducci, *Epigrafia Greca* (Rome, I, 1967; II, 1969; III, 1974; IV, 1978)

L.H. Jeffery, *The Local Scripts of Archaic Greece* (Oxford 1961; 2nd edn by A.W. Johnston 1990)

A.G. Woodhead, *The Study of Greek Inscriptions* (2nd edn, Cambridge 1959)

3 *Pots and potsherds*
HAROLD B. MATTINGLY

A. SOME EARLY LETTERING

The earliest examples of written alphabetic Greek are found on pottery vessels. From *ca.* 700 BC comes the famous cup from Ischia (Pithekousai), written in the script of the first Greek colony, Kyme (p. **30**). Three lines run from right to left as in Phoenician. The first says: 'I am the cup of Nestor, which is good to drink from.' It is followed by a verse couplet: 'Whoever drinks from me will immediately be seized by desire for Aphrodite of the fair crown.' A cup of about 650 BC from Attica is much more modest, saying only 'I am the cup of Tharrias' (fig. **1**). Nearer 600 BC and also from Attica is the *boustrophedon* graffito 'Egestratos (gave me) to Haisimon' (fig. **2**)—one of a group from the Hymettos region, some of which may represent an early method of voting, like the later ostraka, to which we shall presently turn.

Sometimes a more prestigious material than pot was chosen. Fig. **3a–b** shows a gold phiale dedicated at Olympia from the spoils of Heracleia in Acarnania, probably rather after 600 BC. Kypselos, the dedicator, was the first tyrant of Corinth, who set up his sons as subordinate rulers in the islands and mainland of north-west Greece. The script is archaic Corinthian; it features the letter *koppa* (ϙ) in the name Kypselidai—the letter survived until just after 480 BC, and was retained on the coinage for the ethnic K(orinthion); see Chapter 4, fig. **3**.

1   Attic cup, *ca.* 650 BC.

2   Graffito, Attica, *ca.* 600 BC.

3a–b   Gold phiale, after 600 BC.

4 Etruscan helmet.

Another dedication from Olympia a century later is an Etruscan helmet with the inscription 'Hieron son of Deinomenes and the Syracusans (dedicated this) to Zeus, Etruscan spoils from Kyme' (fig. **4**). In 474 the tyrant of Syracuse won a renowned naval battle at Kyme against the Etruscans. *Kappa* is used instead of *koppa*; it is found on Syracusan coins from *ca*. 480 BC.

Inscriptions could be painted on the pot before firing, rather than incised. A Laconian pot of *ca*. 550 BC found at Vulci in Etruria shows King Arkesilaos II of Cyrene presiding over the valuable export wool being weighed and loaded on to ships (fig. **5**). (The scene was once wrongly thought to portray the export of the mysterious herb silphion.) The characters are labelled (the names include Arkesilas, Sophortios and Sliphomachos), and there are even snatches of conversation—*stathmos* ('weight') and *oryxon* ('haul') must be cries. The cup is invaluable evidence for the development of the Laconian script, since it can be closely dated on historical grounds.

The Attic black-figure cup of *ca*. 540–530 BC comes from Tarentum, another centre of the wool industry (fig. **6**). The dedicatory inscription runs: 'Melousa won it as a prize in a girls' competition for carding wool.'

In time, pottery as a writing surface was used for a wide variety of purposes: for school exercises, for lists and messages, for noting ownership, for marking the price, weight or volume of a jar or the nature of its contents (wine, oil, honey, etc.). In Athens, painters' and potters' signatures could be added to vases before firing, or invocations to a boy favourite ('Leagros kalos'); the latter are occasionally found inscribed when the pot was in use. Some of these messages on pot are now baffling, but the ones in the next group are clear enough.

5 Laconian cup, *ca.* 550 BC.

6 Attic black-figure cup (base), *ca.* 540-30 BC.

B. THE STORY OF THE OSTRAKA (487-416 BC)

The best material for studying shifts in script and spelling and the varying degrees of literacy in ancient Greek society comes from fifth-century Athens. Threatened by Persia after the surprising victory of Marathon in 490 BC, Athens devised a neat method for getting rid of powerful potential traitors. Any year the people could decide to hold an 'ostracism'. If it was so decided, the people met in the Agora and voted against prominent politicians by inscribing a name on a piece of pot (*ostrakon*). The man with most votes—as long as 6,000 voted— had to go into exile for ten years, but kept his civil rights and property. Though some returned from this form of exile, ostracism normally finished a political career. From the late 470s onwards ostracism was increasingly used against politicians considered too ambitious or too controversial for the smooth working of the democratic system. But for nearly seventy years Athens used ostracism moderately: only eight certain victims are known. We now have well over 12,000 ostraka from the Agora and the Kerameikos. Some of them carry additional abusive remarks, some caricatures.

On the reverse of the sherd with the drawing of a rider on a horse (fig. **7a–c**) we find the inscription '[Me]gakles son of Hippokrates and Koisyra'. The ostracism of Megakles was in 486 BC; we know of Koisyra, his father's Eretrian mistress, from Aristophanes, two generations later. Since Megakles' string of race-horses is attacked on another sherd, we may be sure that the drawing is also hostile— pointing to him as the typical would-be tyrant.

Sometimes the voter used part of the decoration of a fine vase to make his point. In fig. **8a–b**, the fallen man under the fragment of Megakles' name (of it we can read -]*s Hippokra* [-) graphically foretells Megakles' impending ruin. Another

7a Potsherd used as ostrakon.
b-c Drawings of both sides.

26

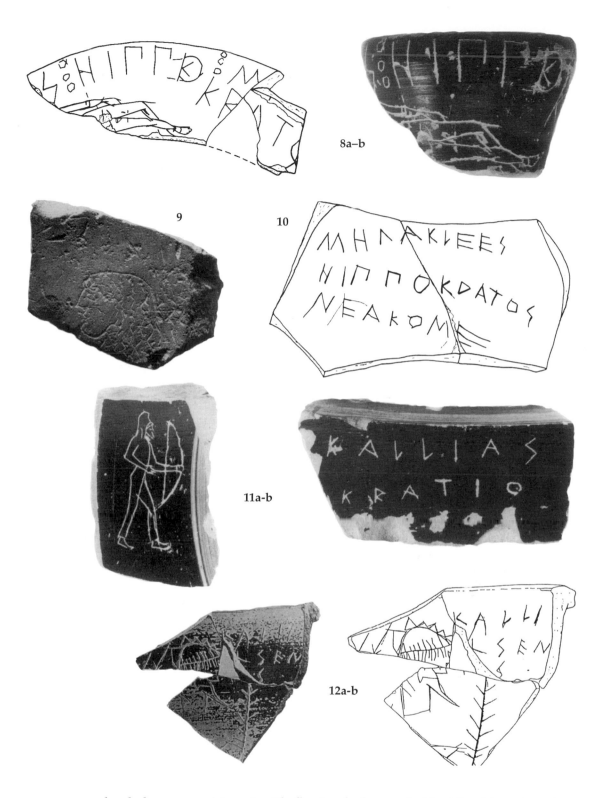

8a–b

9

10

11a-b

12a-b

sherd shows an aristocrat with flowing locks—probably Megakles, since two other ostraka (figs. **9–10**) mock him for his new hairstyle (*nea kome*): long hair characterised men at Athens who admired Sparta or aspired to tyranny. At the same ostracism as Megakles, Kallias son of Kratias was attacked by voters as pro-Persian (*Medos*) and one sherd shows him as a Persian archer (fig. **11a–b**). Fifteen years later the Persian slur was still very powerful: Kallixenos son of Aristonymos was called a 'traitor' (*prodotes*) and another sherd links his name with a caricature of the Great King of Persia with his distinctive cockscomb crown (fig. **12a-b**).

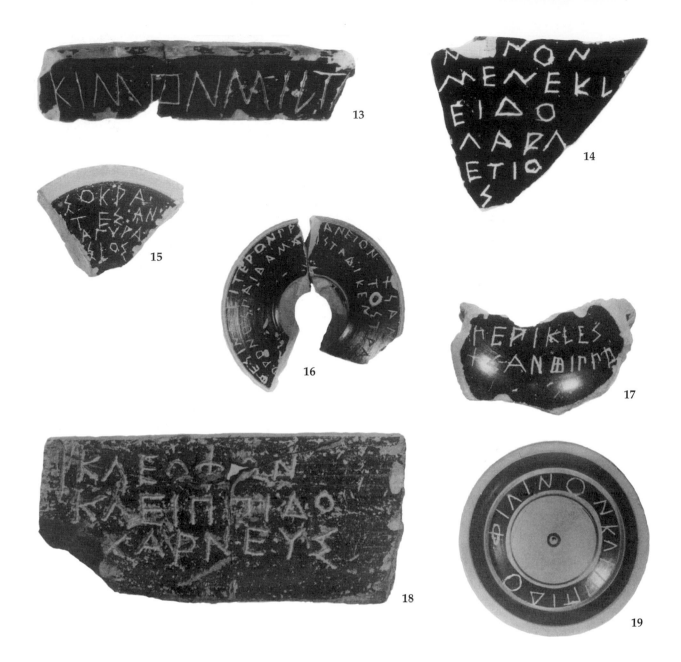

The writing on ostraka shows great variety, as does the spelling. The script can be very square and rather old-fashioned, as with the sherd against Kimon in 461 BC (fig. **13**); or it can be neat with the name distributed in six lines (Menon, 461 BC: fig. **14**); or curiously jumbled (Sokrates, a general *ca.* 440 BC, not the philosopher: fig. **15**). One voter composed two abusive verses against Xanthippos in 484 BC ('worst of the accursed magistrates': fig. **16**), but, though he *was* ostracised, he came back under amnesty in four years to fight the Persians. Only two sherds are known against his son Perikles. One (fig. **17**) is curiously old-fashioned for *ca.* 440 BC, when it was probably cast.

Any piece of pot, tile or brick could serve the voters. A broken tile (fig. **18**) was used against the demagogue Kleophon in 416 BC. Much neater is the vote against his brother Philinos (fig. **19**), on a cup-base (like many others). The votes against these brothers have proved that, far from being the social upstarts of a hostile tradition, they were sons of Kleidippides of Acharnai, a contemporary and political ally of Perikles. Many votes were cast against him *ca.* 440 BC, when Perikles' great rival Thukydides son of Melesias was ostracised.

20   21   22   23

In 416 BC a blatant attempt to gang up against Alkibiades and Phaiax was foiled when they combined forces and engineered the ostracism of the demagogue Hyperbolos instead. This affair so discredited ostracism that it was never used again. But the tactics then employed were not so new in themselves, only the extent and the blatancy. We have evidence, in sherds written by the same hand or pre-prepared by being painted on the pot, that political claques processed sherds for distribution to the voters. The most striking evidence comes from a cache of 192 ostraka against Themistokles, which were written by only fourteen hands. Figs. **20–3** show two of the clearest of these groups. (Themistokles is spelled throughout with two *thetas*, always of the 'hot-cross bun' variety; on **20–1** the *mu* is oversize compared with the other letters and the *kappa* small, while on **22–3** the *mu* is small and the *kappa* large.) If there were any doubt about their purpose, the second group adds the terse order *ito* ('get out').

Some of the sherds written, like these, in one hand may after all be innocent enough. The great statesman Aristeides was once asked by an illiterate Athenian to write the name Aristeides for him. 'Why do you want Aristeides out?' he asked. 'Because I am tired of hearing him called the Just', was the reply. Clearly some voters may have been motivated by such odd reasoning as this. But the requirement of a majority from a quorum of 6,000 (a higher number than ever attended the Assembly otherwise) was designed to ensure that no one would be ostracised on unfair or trivial grounds.

SOME FURTHER READING

L.H. Jeffery, *The Local Scripts of Archaic Greece* (Oxford 1961; 2nd edn by
    A.W. Johnston 1990)
M.L. Lang, *Graffiti and Dipinti. The Athenian Agora* 21 (Princeton 1976)
M.L. Lang, *Ostraka. The Athenian Agora* 25 (Princeton 1990)
H.B. Mattingly, 'The practice of ostracism at Athens', *Antichthon* 25 (1991) 1–26
E. Vanderpool, 'Ostracism at Athens', in C. G. Boulter *et al.*, eds, *Lectures in Memory
    of Louise Taft Semple*, Second Series, 1966–70 (University of Cincinnati Classical
    Studies II, Norman, Oklahoma 1973) 215–70

'Nestor's cup', ca. 700 BC: see p. 23 above.

ILLUSTRATIONS

1 Jeffery, pl. 1.4   **2** Jeffery, pl. 2.9c   **3a–b** Jeffery, pl. 19.13   **4** Ian Carradice, *Greek Coins* (London 1995), fig. 14   **5** after P. Arias, M. Hirmer and B.B. Shefton, *History of Greek Vase Painting* (London 1962), pls. 74 and XXIV   **6** Jeffery, pl. 53.1   **7-11, 12b** *Athenische Mitteilungen* 107 (1992), 161–83   **12a** *Hesperia* 19 (1950), pl. 112, no. 29 (Stamires and Vanderpool)   **13–14** *Athenische Mitteilungen* 80 (1965) Beilage 36.2 and 36.7 (Willemsen)   **15** Lang, *Ostraka*, pl. 3. 661   **16–17** Ibid. pl. 3.1065 and 651   **18** *Hesperia* 37 (1968), pl. 34. 6 (Vanderpool)   **19** Lang, *Ostraka*, pl. 3.659   **20–3** Ibid, pls. 4–5 (excerpted)   **'Nestor's cup'** *Cambridge Ancient History*, plates to vol. 3, 2nd edn (Cambridge 1984), 378 (Jeffery)

4 From Phanes to Pisanello:
2000 years of numismatic Greek
T. R. VOLK

1 'Phanes': electrum stater, retrograde Ionic script with 3-bar *sigma* (*obverse*). [3 : 1]

2 Naxos: silver tetradrachm, Chalcidic script with **X** for **Ξ**, and **O** for long 'o' (*reverse*). [1.75 : 1]

'I am the badge of Phanes': this short but remarkable Greek text appears above the image of a grazing stag on an electrum stater (standard-unit) now in the British Museum (fig. **1**). The formula, which has a parallel on a scarab-seal from Aegina, could hardly have been more explicit. In naming the 'owner' of the pictorial type, it fulfils the most fundamental of the purposes for which language is used on coins: to identify the authority responsible for issuing the currency, and so guaranteeing its value for subsequent transactions. The need for such a guarantee was especially important where (as here) the intrinsic value of the metal, an alloy of gold and silver, was not easily ascertained. Where that authority corresponded to a people rather than a single individual, the term commonly employed for such expressions is 'ethnic'.

Secondary uses of coin-inscriptions or 'legends' vary both by place and by period, with their increasing complexity a reflection of the ever-wider use of coin; and perhaps, too, of an ever-wider (if somewhat basic) level of literacy. They include dating an issue either by the names of city-magistrates or by year-numbers; indicating the denomination; and naming the mint or workshop, the official or magistrate charged with its production, and even, on rare occasions, the engraver. Although often normalised in modern printed catalogues, the Greek of these legends is similarly varied. A number of early issues preserve regional scripts or dialect forms, traces of which continue to appear on coins struck well into the classical period, seemingly as 'heraldic' archaisms. Other issues serve to document and even to date the evolution of individual letter-shapes.

Except for the archaic period, when Greek coins were in effect unifaced, legends were until imperial times generally confined to the reverse. A major challenge of coin-design is to create a harmonious balance between text and pictorial type. One of the most successful examples is found on a silver tetradrachm (4-drachma coin) of Naxos (Sicily) of the mid-fifth century (fig. **2**), where the placement of the short ethnic **NAXION** ('of [the] Naxians') about the figure of a squatting

3   Corinth: silver tridrachm (stater), with initial *koppa* (*obverse*). [2 : 1]

Silenus is made integral to the composition. But the more complex texts of later times often sit rather awkwardly with their pictorial types, and may even have been the work of different sets of engravers.

The legend of the 'Phanes' coin, **ΦΑ[?]ΝΟΣ ΕΜΙ ΣΕΜΑ**, is written in Ionic Greek (here normalised). It appears as mirror-writing: i.e. retrograde letters running from right to left. The reading of the first word is not certain—there may be another letter between the *alpha* and the *nu;* but an electrum *trite*, or third of a stater, with the same grazing stag type has the legend **ΦΑΝΕΟΣ** ('of Phanes'). When and where the stater was made is far from clear. An 'early' date is suggested by the fabric: the use of electrum, the oblong shape, and the three punchmarks comprising the reverse 'type'. The coin was acquired in 1825 at Izmir (Turkey), with the information that it had been found further down the coast at Bodrum, the ancient Halicarnassus. It is therefore tempting to identify the 'Phanes' of the coin either with Phanes (Φάνης), the Halicarnassian mercenary of the second half of the sixth century whom Herodotus (*Histories* 3.4) places first in Egyptian and then in Persian service; or possibly with his grandfather. Personal names on coins of this date are extremely rare—the closest parallel is provided by three 'Lydian' issues—and it is possible that such pieces were produced by individuals in a private capacity.

Legends of any kind on early Greek coins are the exception rather than the rule. The island of Aegina was by ancient tradition the first state of Greece proper to issue a coinage. Her silver *chelonai* ('turtles/tortoises') were sufficiently recognisable throughout the Aegean by the *sema* furnishing their nickname to require no textual reinforcement until the latter part of the fourth century. A rare ethnic from the Greek homeland is that of Corinth: her earliest issues (silver tridrachms, or 3-drachma pieces, from the second half of the sixth century) have as their obverse type an image of Pegasus below which appears the single letter ϙ, the original initial of the city's name (fig. **3**). Not only does this combination of Pegasus and *koppa* serve as Corinth's numismatic *sema* until Hellenistic times, and therefore long after ϙ had been replaced by **K** (*kappa*) for other purposes, but it provided the model for coins issued in the names of a number of Corinthian colonies, such as Leucas (Pegasus and **Λ**) and Ambracia (Pegasus and **A**).

One area that used written ethnics from the start of its coinage was Magna Graecia. There the various Achaean colonies on the Ionic Gulf, together with their secondary foundations, issued a silver coinage quite unlike that of any other ancient series in its appearance. This so-called incuse coinage was struck from pairs of complementary dies, the image on the punch or reverse tool comprising either a back-view of that of the obverse or a direct copy. In either case, the design on the punch was cut in relief, rather than counter-sunk in the normal way, so that when the two dies were correctly aligned the resulting striking gave an unusual

4a–b   Poseidonia: silver stater, Achaean script
with **M** (*san*) for Σ (*obverse* & *reverse*). [1.25 : 1]

double-view of the type, one in relief, the other in intaglio. The singularity of the
series is underlined by the use of strong decorative patterns to provide a border;
and it is not to be excluded that at least at the beginning, the different cities pro-
ducing these incuse coins employed the same group of engravers.

Issues of the first period of incuse coinage, though weighing less than Corinthian
tridrachms, were struck on flans (the uncoined metal disks) distinctive for their
thinness and breadth. The broad flans offered the die-cutter the space to produce lettering that was several times the height of that shown on the 'Phanes'
coin. Clean, single strokes with an engraving tool give an elegant, if somewhat
angular, script, whose local forms such as **M** (*san*) for Σ were to outlive the incuse
fabric. The legends themselves, often repeated on the reverse, generally com-
prise the first two, three, or four letters of the ethnic, e.g. **META** (Metapontum),
Ϙ**PO** (Croton), **MY** (Sybaris), the last providing a *terminus ante quem* of 510 BC, the
year of the city's destruction by Croton. The text may read from left to right or
right to left, or even a mixture of the two, with individual letters reversed.

Quite why the colonies of Magna Graecia should have been so emphatic in their
use of ethnics is not immediately obvious. The hoard-evidence suggests that the
circulation of these early issues, especially the slightly lighter coins of
Poseidonia (fig. **4a-b**), a secondary settlement on the northern coast of Lucania,
was very restricted; and the pictorial types of the main settlements are strikingly
different from one another, e.g. a corn-ear at Metapontum, a tripod at Croton,
and Poseidon at Poseidonia. The letters of the legend perhaps served as much to
affirm or to project the 'Greekness' of the issuing city in a largely non-Hellenic
environment, as to guarantee the coin's worth. Indeed, the appearance of the
coinage of the Western Greeks as a whole is remarkable for its adventurousness
compared with that of Greece proper. Certain issues of Sicilian cities from the
end of the fifth century, long counted among the most beautiful of the Greek
world, carry the signatures of their engravers, e.g. **EΞAKIΣTIΔAΣ** at Camarina,
HPAKΛEIΔAΣ at Catana and **KIMΩN** at Syracuse. Usually cut in microscopic
letters (presumably with the aid of a rock-crystal lens), they are often ingeniously
concealed within the detail of the type.

During the second half of the fifth century, the dominant coin of the Greek
homelands, and beyond, was the silver tetradrachm of Athens (fig. **5**). Produced
in what were by the standards of pre-Hellenistic Greece massive numbers, it was
some 40 per cent heavier than the Aeginetan 'turtle' and twice the weight of the
Corinthian unit. It served both as an important export-commodity, by adding to
the value of the silver extracted from the Laurion mines; and as a political instrument, by means of the so-called 'currency' decree of the 420s by which Athens
sought to impose her coins, weights, and measures on the allied states of the

5 Athens: silver tetradrachm, 'owl' series, with dotted *theta* and *epsilon* for the long 'e' (reverse). [2 : 1]

6 Athens: silver tetradrachm, *stephanephoros* ('wreathed') or 'New-style' (*reverse*). [2 : 1]

Delian League. The origin of the coinage is advertised by its pictorial types: the head of Athena on the obverse, and on the reverse, the standing owl from which the coins derived their popular sobriquet of *glaukes* ('owls') and which was a device of the goddess herself. But unlike the earliest coins of Athens, the so-called 'Wappenmünzen' with their variable badges, from the very first issue, some time after the expulsion of Hippias in 510, the 'owl' coinage carried the unmistakable reverse signature **AΘE**(ναιον). The presence of the ethnic is a reminder that Athena was by no means an exclusively Athenian deity, and it seems hardly coincidental that about this time Corinth replaced the formerly typeless reverse of the Pegasus series with her own version of the goddess' head.

At Athens, the ethnic is boldly placed in the manner of the southern Italian incuse coinage. But the method of inscribing the letters is rather different. Instead of single strokes, the ends of the letters are first marked by drill-holes and the arms then incised as a linear cut, a technique common to the whole of the city's later precious-metal coinage. The original orthography, where *epsilon* is used for both the short and (as here) long forms of the 'e' vowel-sound, was not abandoned until the second century AD, by which time production had been limited to bronze issues. Athenian conservatism regarding the city's signature is usually explained as a function of the tetradrachm's rôle as a trade/commodity coinage.

'Owl' tetradrachms, often of crude manufacture, continued to be issued well into the Hellenistic period. A replacement coinage, the so-called 'New-style' issues, had to wait until some thirty years after the 'liberation' of Greece by the Roman general T. Flamininus in 196 BC. The classic types of Athena and standing owl remain, though dramatically reworked; but the much broader and flatter flans of Hellenistic type become in due course the vehicles for a mass of written information. Thus on a typical reverse of the 90s BC the ethnic appears in a subsidiary position, above the names of two annual magistrates, **ΝΙΚΗΤΗΣ** and **ΔΙΟΝΥΣΙΟΣ** (fig. 6). Also shown are a variable year-symbol (Gorgoneion), one of eight other personal names, here **ΞΕ(ΝΟ)**, belonging to an official holding office for part of the year, the month of production (**H** = month 7), and a set of variable control-letters (**MH**) perhaps indicating the metal-source. Apart from the frozen formula **AΘE**, these texts show no inhibition over the use of either *eta* or *omega* forms to indicate the long vowel forms.

7 Macedon, Alexander III:
silver tetradrachm, with
monogram below throne
(*reverse*). [2 : 1]

A feature of Hellenistic coins, including Athenian 'New-style' issues of the early
period, is the use of monograms. These 'privy' marks, related to mint or financial administration, are not always easy to resolve. In general, they can be seen
as a function of the new political geography brought about by the conquests of
Alexander the Great (336–323 BC) and in particular the creation of what were
essentially a number of uniform coinages. Of these, the most important were the
tetradrachms of Alexander-type, issued over a period of more than two centuries by a multiplicity of city-regimes, some identified by state-monograms,
others by symbols based on their traditional devices. But in most cases, the
marks serve to distinguish the issues of the different 'magistrates', whether
mint-officials or financial officers, operating at each centre of production.

More than 850 different monograms are to be found on Alexander-type
tetradrachms, either singly or in groups of two or even three. Thus on an issue
from the king's lifetime probably struck at Myriandros (later called Alexandria
ad Issum, Syria), the monogram **M I**(?) is sometimes read as the mint's signature
(fig. **7**). The ankh symbol in the field to the left of the standard type of a seated
Zeus is one of five secondary devices, including second monograms, to appear
with this signature.

The Macedonian empire and its successor states were responsible for greatly
extending the use of 'Greek'-style coins. Most remarkable was their influence on
the coinage of the Indian subcontinent. During the course of the second century
the Greek-ruled kingdom of Bactria, to the south of the Hindu Kush, expanded
into what is now south-eastern Afghanistan and northern Pakistan. For more
than a century thereafter, various Indo-Greek kingdoms struck silver and base-
metal bilingual coins. Thus on a mid-second century silver tetradrachm of
Menander I Soter the Kharoshthi legend (*menaṃdrasa maharajasa fratarasa*) on the
reverse is equivalent to the Greek text (ΜΕΝΑΝΔΡΟΥ ΒΑΣΙΛΕΩΣ ΣΩΤΗΡΟΣ)
encircling the royal portrait (fig. **8a-b**).

8a–b Bactria, Menander I Soter:
silver tetradrachm, bilingual issue
(*obverse* & *reverse*). [1.5 : 1]

9 Parthia, Phraates IV: silver drachm, with square-cut letters (*reverse*). [2 : 1]

In the meantime, a powerful new state had emerged in what had previously been a part of the Seleucid kingdom. Ruled by the descendants of Arsaces, a Scythian chieftain, Parthia had by the middle of the second century BC come to occupy much of the land on either side of the modern border between Iraq and Iran. Among the Hellenised institutions inherited by the Arsacids was a 'Greek' coinage that survived until the early third century AD. The script of the later issues is characterised by a sharp, angular style that by the middle of the first century BC often leads to the adoption of a square *sigma* and, as here, a simple + for Φ (fig. **9**).

Roman domination of the East did not lead to a significant fall in the frequency of Greek coin-inscriptions for at least two centuries. Although Latin was used on the coinage of Roman colonial foundations, Greek was still the language of most 'provincial' issues. The number and volume of these coinages varied greatly: some cities struck regularly, others on just one or two occasions. Except for 'semi-autonomous' issues, the obverse type normally comprised the head of the emperor or of a member of his family, accompanied by an identifying legend. In general, these texts avoid the complexities of imperial titulature often displayed on contemporary state coins and consist of a transliteration of the ruler's name and a translation into Greek of the basic elements of his title. Thus *imperator* becomes *autokrator* and *Augustus* becomes *Sebastos*. Reference to the locality, usually in the form of a complete ethnic in the genitive plural, appears on the reverse, together with an appropriate pictorial type.

Among changes in letter-forms registered on issues of imperial times is an increasing tendency to employ Є for E and C for Σ, the latter already occasionally found on Athenian 'New-style' coins as early as the second century BC. At Smyrna (Asia), the introduction of the lunate forms of *sigma* and *epsilon*—though not invariable thereafter—can be dated to the last decade of the reign of Augustus. A bronze issue of the *strategos* Koronos, honouring Augustus, Tiberius Caesar and Livia (all in the accusative case): **CЄBACTON, TIBЄPION KAICAPA**; heads of Augustus and Tiberius \ **ΛIBIAN**; **ZMYPNAIΩN** (ethnic); **KOPΩNOC** (magistrate); standing figure of Aphrodite Stratonikis (a local cult), to whom perhaps Livia is here assimilated (fig. **10a-b**).

10a-b Smyrna, Koronos, *ca.* AD 4–14: bronze issue (*obverse & reverse*). [2 : 1]

11 Anastasius I: copper 40-nummus (**M**), *officina* Δ (*reverse*). [1.25 : 1]

The last 'provincial' coinage of the Greek East was suppressed by Diocletian at the end of the third century AD, as part of a general reform of the currency. From this point, issues of uniform type were struck at up to sixteen regular state mints located across the empire. The language of these coins was Latin, but even so the use of Greek was not wholly lost. In the West each workshop (*officina*) within a particular mint normally marked its production either by the appropriate initial letter, **P**(*rima*), **S**(*ecunda*), **T**(*ertia*) or **Q**(*uarta*), or (more rarely) by a Roman numeral; mints in the East used Greek letters in their numeric guise. Thus at Antioch (Syria), where the number of *officinae* had by 311–313 risen to fifteen, the sequence ran from **A** to **ЄI**. There was, however, a notable exception. Since the end of the previous century, when the total of workshops was raised to ten, the ninth *officina* employed the formula **ΔЄ** (i.e. 4 + 5) thus avoiding the number **Θ** with its connotation of *thanatos* ('death'). The inhibition does not appear to have outlived state recognition of Christianity, since by 330-333 the use of **Θ** is normal.

Although after the fall of the Western empire in 476 Latin continued to be the language of state, that hardly reflected day-to-day reality at Constantinople. As early as Anastasius' reform of the coinage in 498, the Greek character of the empire was recognised by the prominent use of the numerals **M**, **K**, **I**, and (from a second reform in 512) **Є**, to indicate (respectively) the values of 40, 20, 10, and 5 nummi (fig. 11). By the first quarter of the ninth century, the imperial titulature presents an inextricable mix of Latin and Greek forms: Greek titles such as *basileus* are transliterated into Latin script, and Latin digraphs are replaced by their Greek equivalents (e.g. **TH** by **Θ** in the name Theophilus [**ΘЄOFILOS**]).

What is perhaps the most bizarre example of the mixing of Greek and Latin had already occurred on a series of gold solidi struck by Leo IV (775–780): to accompany portraits of the emperor, his son (Constantine VI), his grandfather (Leo III) and his father (Constantine V), a lengthy Greek text detailing the relationships is (more or less) transliterated into Latin script (fig. **12a-b**): **LЄON VS S ЄCCON CONSTANTINOS O NЄOS** (= Λέων υἱὸς καὶ ἔγγονος Κωνσταντῖνος ὁ νέος, 'Leo son and grandson, Constantine the younger')\ **LЄON PAP' CONSTANTINOS PATHR** (Λέων πάππος Κωνσταντῖνος πατήρ, 'Leo grandfather, Constantine father').

12a-b Leo IV: gold solidus, so-called 'family' issue (*obverse & reverse*). [1.5 : 1]

13 Pisanello: cast bronze portrait medal
of John VIII Palaeologus (*obverse*). [1 : 1]

Our best example of a contemporary Greek numismatic inscription setting out
the name and style of a Byzantine emperor dates to the fifteenth century.
This is the cast medal made by Antonio Pisano (di Puccio), known as
Pisanello (*ca.* 1395–1455), to record the visit to Italy that John VIII Palaeologus
made as part of an ill-fated attempt to secure the reunion of the Eastern and
Western Churches (fig. **13**). The work was undertaken either during the imperial
entourage's residence at Ferrara in 1438 or after the ecumenical council's trans-
fer to Florence early the following year.

The obverse legend reads: +ΙѠÁΝΝΗС·ΒΑСΙΛΕ῁Ϲ·ΚΑῚ·ΑΥΤΟ=ΚΡÁΤѠΡ·
ΡѠΜÁΙѠΝ·Ο·ΠΑΛΑΙΟΛÓΓΟϹ; the reverse includes the artist's signature in
both Greek and Latin. The script, complete with diacritics and punctuated in
the manner of early imperial coins, is testimony as much to humanist taste as to
Byzantine diplomatics. Yet it comes just as Western scholars of the like of
Ambrogio Traversari and Ciriaco de' Pizzicolli (Cyriac of Ancona) were beginning to recognise the difference between the Greek hands of their day and the
vetustissimae literae graecae and *atticae literae* used to cut the legends of Hellenistic
coins.

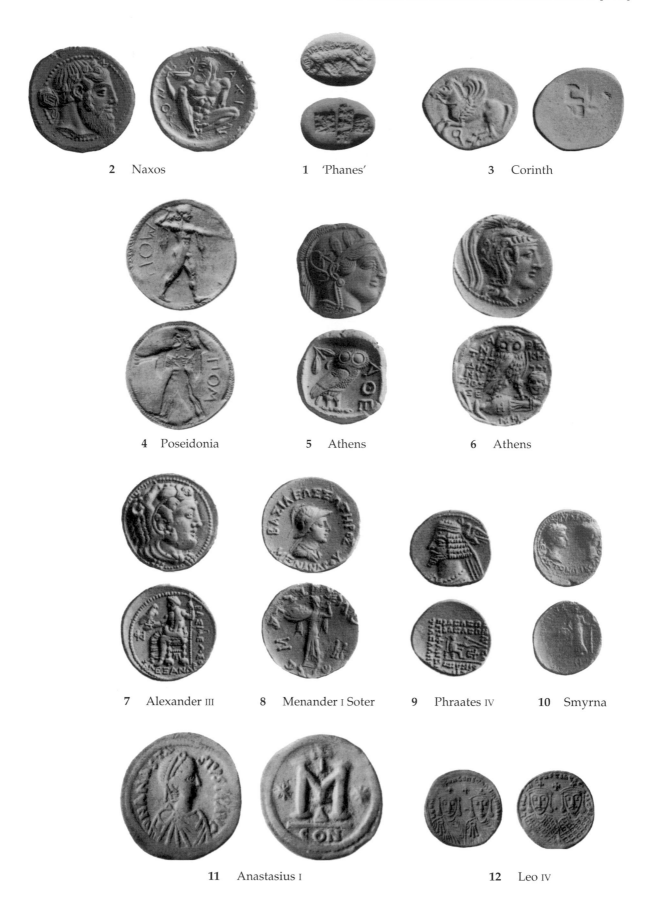

2   Naxos   **1**   'Phanes'   **3**   Corinth

4   Poseidonia   **5**   Athens   **6**   Athens

7   Alexander III   **8**   Menander I Soter   **9**   Phraates IV   **10**   Smyrna

11   Anastasius I   **12**   Leo IV

SOME FURTHER READING

Although their information on coin-dates is often obsolete, the essays by J.E. Hartmann and Sir George Macdonald reproduced in *Greek Numismatic Epigraphy* (Chicago 1969) are still useful. There is much detailed information, including remarks on scripts in the Roman and Byzantine periods, in Ernest Babelon's *Traité de monnaies grecques et romaines*, I. *Théorie et doctrine* (Paris 1901). *Coinage in the Greek World* by Ian Carradice and Martin Price (London 1988) provides an excellent introduction to Greek coinage down to Hellenistic times. Greek-language issues under the Roman empire feature in a companion volume by Kevin Butcher, *Roman Provincial Coins: An Introduction to the 'Greek Imperials'* (London 1988). The development of later letter-forms can be followed in the numerous illustrations to Philip Whitting's *Byzantine Coins* (London 1973).

ILLUSTRATIONS

1 Asia Minor: 'Phanes', electrum stater, Halicarnassus (?) (Caria) mint, *ca.* 600–*ca.* 550 BC, or later (Head 1881, pl. 1: 7)

2 Sicily: Naxos, silver tetradrachm, *ca.* 460 BC (*McClean* 1, pl. 83: 8)

3 Southern Italy (Lucania): Poseidonia, silver stater, *ca.* 525–*ca.* 500 BC (*SNG [GB]* 4.1: 535)

4 The Peloponnese (Corinthia): Corinth, silver tridrachm (stater), *ca.* 525–*ca.* 500 BC (*SNG [GB]* 4.4: 3314)

5 Central Greece (Attica): Athens, silver tetradrachm, *ca.* 450–*ca.* 425 BC (*McClean* 2, pl. 207: 3)

6 Central Greece (Attica): Athens, silver tetradrachm, *ca.* 98/7 BC (*McClean* 2, pl. 209: 9)

7 Macedon: Alexander III ('the Great', 336–323 BC), silver tetradrachm, Myriandros (?) (Syria) mint, *ca.* 325–*ca.* 323 BC (*McClean* 2, pl. 126: 6)

8 Bactria: Menander I Soter (*ca.* 155–*ca.* 130 BC), silver tetradrachm, uncertain mint, after *ca.* 145(?) BC (*McClean* 3, pl. 361: 12)

9 Parthia: Phraates IV (*ca.* 38–*ca.* 2 BC), silver drachm, Susa (Babylonia) mint (*McClean* 3, pl. 358: 5)

10 Asia (Ionia): Smyrna, time of Augustus (27BC–AD 14), Koronos (*strategos*), bronze unit (*ca.* 20 mm), *ca.* AD 4–14 (*McClean* 3, pl. 287:14)

11 Byzantium: Anastasius I (AD 491–518), copper 40-nummus or follis, Constantinople mint, second (heavy) issue, from AD 512 (*BMCByz* 1, pl.1: 9)

12 Byzantium: Leo IV (AD 775–780), gold solidus, Constantinople mint, AD 776–778 (*BMCByz* 2, pl. 45: 20)

13 Antonio Pisano (di Puccio), Pisanello, *ca.* 1395–1455: cast bronze portrait-medal of John VIII Palaeologus, 1438 or 1439-40 (*BMCByz* 2, frontispiece).

BMCByz = W. Wroth, *Catalogue of the Imperial Byzantine Coins in the British Museum*, 2 vols. (London 1908)

Head = B.V. Head, A *Guide to the Principal Gold and Silver Coins of the Ancients (Synopsis of the contents of the British Museum)* (London 1881)

McClean = S.W. Grose, *Catalogue of the McClean Collection of Greek Coins, Fitzwilliam Museum*, 3 vols. (Cambridge 1923–1929)

SNG [GB] 4 = F.M. Heichelheim, *Sylloge Nummorum Graecorum. Fitzwilliam Museum: Leake and General Collections*, fasc. 1 (London 1940); fasc. 4 (London 1956)

5 Scribes and scholars
Greek papyri and the survival of literature
ERIC HANDLEY

Clay, stone; wood, metal; sherds of broken pottery—all these materials and others, as this book shows, could carry writing in different periods, places and circumstances in ancient Greece. As literacy spread, papyrus became the main means of written communication; and so it was to be for many centuries. We can say that it was the equivalent of paper in modern societies, but only if we think away the revolution that has come about with the massive growth of printing. Socrates was probably not untypical of his generation of Athenians in the primacy he gave to the spoken word over the book. The book, it seems, began its career as a power in Western society in the latter part of the fifth century BC and the early fourth century; it is from the later years of that century that the earliest examples of Greek books survive. Fig. **1**, though about a hundred years later still, can perhaps be used to give a fair idea of the style and format of its forebears in classical times.

1 Menander, *Sikyonioi,*
third century BC.

3 A group of
papyrus rolls.

2   The structure of
a sheet of papyrus.

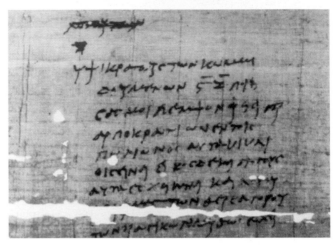

4   A scholar asks for
books, *ca.* AD 170.

Papyrus is made from the pith of a reed, *Cyperus papyrus*, the source of supply
and manufacture being Egypt, where it once grew on the margins of the Nile
much more abundantly than it now does. With the green outer layer removed,
strips or panels of pith are carefully peeled off; a sheet of strips is laid out on a
flat surface, a second sheet is laid on top of it with the fibres at right angles; pres-
sure bonds the two together with the aid of the natural juice of the reed; when
dry, the sheet is trimmed, smoothed, and can be joined with others to make a roll
of the length needed. Fig. **3** shows examples. Fig. **2** illustrates the structure of
the material, with the aid of a modern piece made for the purpose and lit from
behind. The best ancient specimens are cream-coloured, or a pale biscuit-brown,
with fine, regular fibres; for preference, one writes along, not across them; but
fig. **7** is one of very many examples of the back of a roll being used, with the
writing running across, not along, the fibres: a document that was no longer
needed has been turned over and used to copy another text. In a codex (see figs.
6 and **9–10**) the sheets are folded, and both sides are used for writing; by folding
successive sheets in opposite directions, groups or gatherings of leaves can be
made so that the fibres on facing pages match.

Scribes and Scholars is the title of a much admired study to be mentioned below
among suggestions for further reading. Its title is borrowed here to help make
the point that Greek authors of the ancient world are alive today in their own
language and in many others because for generation after generation their writings were meticulously copied by hand, and kept alive not simply by waves of
popular demand, but by study and elucidation in a long, if sometimes thin,
chain of tradition.

The vast majority of our texts come not directly from ancient papyri, but from
their descendants in the shape of manuscript copies of medieval and
Renaissance times. A vast amount of writing has failed to survive. Sophocles,
for example, is credited with writing over 120 plays, of which we have seven
from medieval copies, plus quotations by ancient authors from plays now lost,

Ancient pens were typically made of dried reed, rather than metal or quills. They could be fine or broad at the tip, hard or soft; they wore quite quickly in use on papyrus, and so often needed to be refashioned or replaced. Writing done with a worn nib may look rather different from that done with a fresh one.

Anyone who has used a modern calligraphic pen, or perhaps a felt-tip marker, will know what a great difference can be made to lettering by the angle at which the tip of the writing instrument meets the surface. See the inset figure above. The thin strokes are produced as the pen moves in line with the flat of the nib (in our figure at an angle of about 30 degrees from the vertical); the broad strokes are made when it moves at right angles to that, in line with the stem. A pen so held will tend to make elliptical or oval curves for round letters, and will give an interesting contrast of weight to the sloping strokes; a glide at the beginning or at the end of the upright or sloping strokes gives a decorative effect like a serif.

Try the figure as an aid to seeing how the letters are made in the satyr play fragment on this page, and contrast especially the round hand of **6** as well as the different styles and letter-shapes of the other papyri illustrated here.

Ancient inks vary from black to brown; they were most commonly carbon-based and not metallic (early examples of metallic inks in Greek manuscripts are exceedingly rare); once rubbed or abraded, the writing is very difficult to recover.

5a A fragment of a satyr play, second century AD

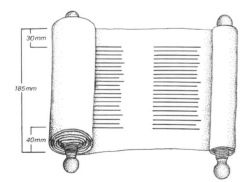

5b A reconstruction of the roll. [Drawing by Sara Owen]

plus fragments of copies on papyrus recovered in modern times: the play illustrated in fig. **5** was probably one of his. The books and pieces of books that survive from the ancient world do so only in special situations. Books are quite fragile objects: they wear out in use, or are neglected and decay; they are easily destroyed by fire or other accident; they suffer malicious damage, not least in war or in acts of oppression.

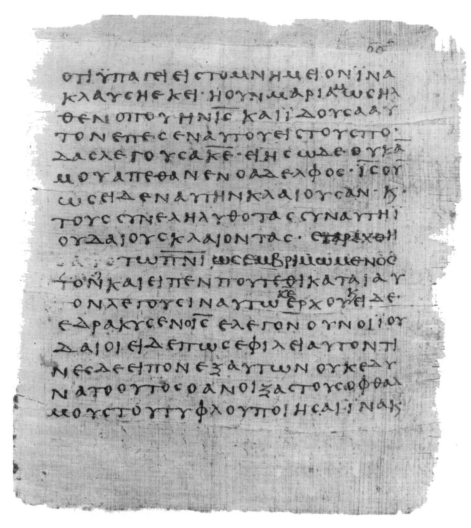

6 Page 79 from a copy of St John's Gospel, third century AD.

Roll and Codex.

Throughout the Classical and the Hellenistic Age, and until the early Roman Imperial period, fair copies of literary texts were made and circulated or sold in the form of rolls. Depictions in vase-paintings tell us what they were like in the time before we have direct evidence from the first surviving examples in the later fourth century BC. The roll was held horizontally in left and right hands and read from left to right. See **5** on the previous page, with the sketch.

Tablets of wood, thin sheets to be written on directly, or else coated with wax which could be smoothed and recycled, were used for drafts, accounts, letters and many other purposes. They could have multiple leaves; in a sense they led the way to the codex of papyrus or prepared animal skin, parchment or vellum — a form of book with superior possibilities for ease of reference, capacity and sheer durability. The two examples illustrated here are the St John's Gospel (left: the codex was much favoured as a vehicle for Christian texts) and the Menander of **9-10**. Some of our earliest evidence comes from epigrams by Martial, who was writing in the later first century AD, when this form of book was a novelty in Rome. It still (so far) survives.

See particularly C. H. Roberts and T. C. Skeat, *The Birth of the Codex* (London 1983)

How is it that any ancient books have survived? Some few, from later antiquity, stayed safe in libraries; some have been found in monastic settlements abandoned and buried by sand, in Egypt's dry climate; one private owner's collection smothered by lava from Vesuvius at Herculaneum is still yielding material; one famous roll, an almost unique survival on the Greek mainland, was discovered in a tomb built over a pyre which had scorched but not consumed it. Often writing material found other uses. Pieces of old books and documents could be used in making bindings for newer books; they could be made into backing for the plaster of mummy cases, as was the roll in fig.**1**; some have been found stuffed into the bodies of mummified ibises and crocodiles. But very often, by their tens and hundreds of thousands, they went for scrap; the rubbish dumps of the city of Oxyrhynchus have yielded to excavations by the Egypt Exploration Society and others papyri which, in the course of a century of work, have filled sixty-four volumes and more. They include the items in figs. **4**, **5**, **7**, **8** and **9**, as well as many pieces larger and better known, both early copies of surviving works and of others otherwise lost.

7 Plato, *Phaedrus*, third century AD.

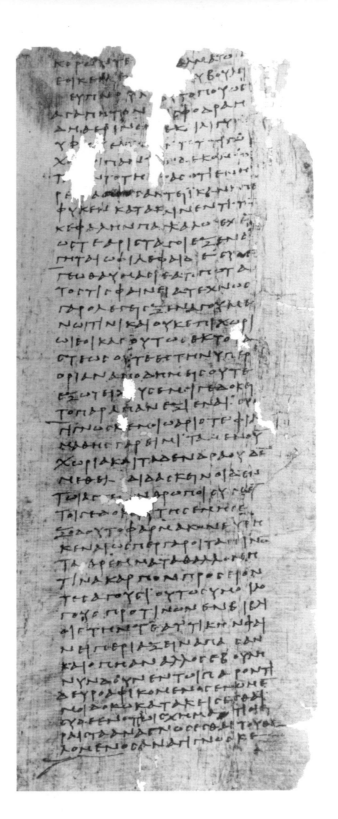

8 An order for payment, AD 307/8.

Together with the books and pieces of them, excavation has recovered countless documents of all kinds—letters, accounts, leases, official decrees and so on. They tell a story of Greek residents, Roman administration and native Egyptians that goes far beyond the brief and limited narrative presented here. One minimal example, put in primarily for comparison with the Plato of fig. **7**, is the private letter of fig. **8**, an order to pay the sum of 1,000 drachmas for wine.

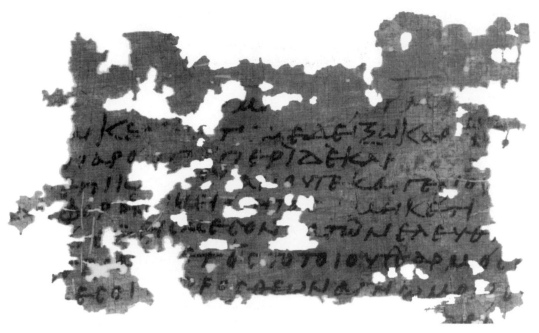

9 Menander, *Aspis,*
sixth century AD.

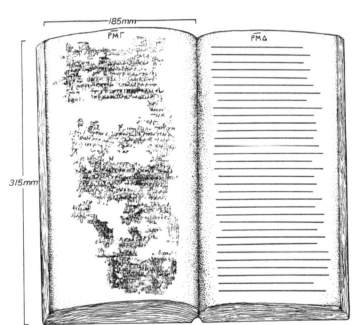

10 Menander, *Aspis* (and other
plays?): sketch for a reconstruction of the codex of **9**.
[Drawing by Sara Owen]

The scribes rarely speak for themselves. One of them does in fig. **1**. Perhaps he
was not only a scribe, but a bookseller in a small way of trade, telling customers
who checked the title and the total of verses at the end of the roll that they
should not be too hard on the writing—or else… Scholars can be more vocal.
We detect their presence behind our texts in minor annotations or corrections;
but sometimes we have extended commentaries, compiled, like their modern
successors, with the aid of earlier work by people who may be cited or criticised.
Fig. **4** shows a specimen of the handwriting of a man busy with his personal
research, who in a postscript to a letter asks his brother for copies of books he
could not find locally. Much though they respect the copyright laws and the
good customs of the photocopier room, many modern scholars make similar
requests to their friends and relations.

SOME FURTHER READING

P.E. Easterling and B.M.W. Knox, 'Books and readers in the Greek world', in *The Cambridge History of Classical Literature* I (1985) 1–41

Italo Gallo, *Greek and Latin Papyrology* (London 1986)

R. Pfeiffer, *A History of Classical Scholarship from the Beginnings to the End of the Hellenistic Age* (Oxford 1968)

L.D. Reynolds and N.G. Wilson, *Scribes and Scholars* (3rd edn, Oxford 1991)

C.H. Roberts, *Greek Literary Hands: 350 BC – AD 400* (Oxford 1955)

E.G. Turner, *Greek Papyri: an introduction* (enlarged edn, Oxford 1980)

E.G. Turner, *Greek Manuscripts of the Ancient World* (2nd edn, 1987) [*GMAW*]

NOTES ON THE ILLUSTRATIONS

1 Paris, Inst. de Papyrologie, *PSorb* inv. 2272–3 (+72), from Ghoran, *ca.* 230-200 BC. Menander, *Sikyonioi*. A column from a roll used as material to make mummy casing, original height about 160 mm. Broken at the right, it gives the end of the play, marked by the *coronis*, a devolved figure of a bird; line-endings from the previous column at the left. Below, title, author's name, total of verses (broken after symbol for 1,000), and then verses by the copyist, μὴ καταγελᾶτε τῆς γραφῆς 'Don't knock the writing…'). Ed. pr. A. Blanchard and A. Bataille, *Rech. de Papyrologie* 3 (1965) 103–76, with facsimile; Turner, *GMAW*, no. 40; Handley, *Pallas* 47 (1997) 186–7.

2 Construction of a sheet of papyrus, after Turner, *GMAW*, no. 77; see also *ibid.*, nos. 1–3, with references.

3 Papyrus rolls from Egypt in Berlin, Staatliche Museen: Turner, *GMAW*, Supplementary Plate II C. Rolls could be fitted with a central wooden spindle, ornamented with knobs, a tag with the title (interesting examples survive), and perhaps a protective wrapper. Catullus xxii has a famous description of a luxury edition of a contemporary Latin poet of the first century BC. See **5**.

4 London, Egypt Exploration Society: *The Oxyrhynchus Papyri*, XVIII (1941), no. 2192 (C. H. Roberts), *ca.* AD 170. A private letter with a postscript about books. The author added greetings to his brother at the end of the fair copy; then, after a false start (deleted, as seen here) he asks, in this rapidly written scholarly hand, for copies of books that he would like to have made and sent, and suggests where they might be found. The first items are Books VI and VII of *People in Comedies* by Hypsikrates, Ὑψικράτους τῶν Κωμῳδουμένων ξζ : 'Harpokration says they are among Polion's books, but it is likely that others own them too'; and he also wants the prose summaries of Thersagoras' *Tragic Myths*. Turner, *GMAW*, no. 68.

5 Cambridge, University Library, MS Add. 5895, from Oxyrhynchus. Sophocles (?). *POxy* VIII 1083 + XVII 2453, second century AD; original height about 185 mm, with generous upper and lower margins. Illustrated here is the largest of many pieces from a group of rolls that represent a scholar's copies of several plays. The playwright is most probably Sophocles; there are scholarly annotations and corrections. The handwriting is professional and calligraphic, upright with oval curves; there is a strong contrast between broad and narrow letters and broad and narrow strokes, the pen being held at a tilt from the horizontal, as in the accompanying diagram. This fragment gives part of a satyr play, in which the Chorus of Satyrs and Oineus (?Phineus, Schoineus) take part. Turner, *GMAW*, no. 28. Text: H. Lloyd-Jones, *Sophocles*, vol. 3 (LCL, 1996) 418–21, with translation and further references; J. Diggle, *Tragicorum Graecorum Fragmenta Selecta* (OCT, 1998) 77–8. Lines 6–7: ἅπαντα πεύσῃ· νυμφίοι μὲν ἥ[κομε]ν Ι παῖδες δὲ νυμφῶν, Βακχίου δ᾽ ὑπηρέται.

6 Geneva, Bibliothèque Bodmer, Pap. II, early third century AD. Gospel according to St John, 1–14. Papyrus codex, with a nearly square format, ht 162 x 142 mm. This page, numbered 79 (o͞θ), has 11: 31 ὅτι ὑπάγει εἰς τὸ μνημεῖον ἵνα Ι κλαύσῃ ἐκεῖ το οὐκ ἐδύ-Ινατο οὗτος ὁ ἀνοίξας τοὺς ὀφθαλ-Ιμοὺς τοῦ τυφλοῦ ποιῆσαι ἵνα κ(αὶ) Ι. The script is a rounded decorated

capital, quite broadly spaced: 'sacred names', in abbreviated form with a bar over them, are typical of Christian texts: I̅C̅ = Ἰησοῦς, K̅E̅ = Κύριε, Π̅N̅I̅ = Πνεύματι. The nature of the corrections (some of which are visible on this page) shows that the text was collated with a copy other than the master from which it was made. Turner, *GMAW*, no. 63.

7   Toledo, Ohio, Museum of Art, from Oxyrhynchus, third century AD. Plato, *Phaedrus* 227A–230E, written on the back of a register of landowners. *POxy* VII 1016 (VII 1044). Papyrus roll, ht 280 mm: six columns of 240 mm containing between 42 and 47 lines each, in a well-written upright hand of the kind often called 'formal mixed', showing accentuated straight strokes and small tight curves, as in ε θ ο ϲ. There are some corrections and accents by a second hand. Col. vi, shown here, reads at its foot: νῦν δ᾽ οὖν ἐν τῶι παρόντι | δεῦρο ἀφικό-μενος ἐγὼ μέ(ν) | μοι δοκῶ κατακείσεσθαι, | σύ δ᾽ ἐν ὁποίωι [corrected from ὅτωι] σχήματι οἴει | ῥᾷιστα ἀναγνώσεσθαι τοῦθ᾽ ἑ-Iλόμενος ἀναγίγνωσκε—|. Up to this point, the text represents the proem of the dialogue, its ending marked by the forked paragraphus at the foot: this excerpt could have been regarded as an entity in itself; but perhaps another roll was used for the continuation. Turner, *GMAW*, no. 84.

8   London, Egypt Exploration Society: *The Oxyrhynchus Papyri* LXI (1995), no. 4123 (T. Gagos), AD 307/8. An order to make a payment, from one Theudas to his brother Ananias, interesting not least because their names are thought likely to indicate that they were members of a Jewish community in early fourth-century Oxyrhynchus. Very few literary papyri can be given precise dates; dated documents like this one, apart from their intrinsic interest, are helpful to set up the criteria of dating by style on which palaeographers so largely depend. Here the comparison with **7** is worth making; the less formal character of the document shows more easily the direction and flow of the strokes that make up the letters: Θευδᾶς Ἀνανίᾳ | ἀδελφῷ χαίρειν|.

9   London, Egypt Exploration Society: *The Oxyrhynchus Papyri* LXI (1995), no. 4094 (E. W. Handley), sixth century AD. Menander, *Aspis* (and other plays?). With the aid of the text given by the Bodmer codex, published in 1969 (*PBodmer* XXVI), this single leaf of a large book was put together by Dr W.E.H. Cockle from numerous broken fragments. One side of the top of it is illustrated here. The page number P̅M̅Γ̅ (=143) is written twice, now damaged both times; there follow the remains of *Aspis* 199ff. The complete page has 33 lines, with 28 on page 142. The height of 315 mm is probably original; the width can be calculated from the text at *ca.* 185–90 mm. The handwriting is a large, sloping and sometimes sprawling majuscule. It is similar in style, as the tall and relatively narrow page is similar in format, to the Cairo codex of Menander, probably to be dated a century or more earlier, whose publication in 1907 was the first major stage of this lost author's continuing recovery. Like the Cairo codex, this book presumably contained a selection of Menander's plays; calculation shows that there would be room for four of average length before *Aspis*. There are corrections (though none that show that a second original was used); there is also occasional and sometimes wrong accentuation, some of this added at the stage of correction. Similar copies of Euripides and others are known from the early Byzantine period, both on papyrus and on its ultimately predominant rival, vellum; and there are remains of a codex of the Septuagint from Oxyrhynchus in a very similar style. Impressive for size rather than for elegance, these volumes seem more suitable for reading from a lectern than for reference and close study; yet the medieval manuscripts on which most of the surviving Greek classics depend must often have had books of this kind among their ancestors, especially when they were recopied in a format which could carry a marginal commentary. Line 205 (the last shown) reads: δοκῶ] δέ σοι τ[ι] πρὸς θεῶν ἀγνωμονεῖ[ν, where ἀγνωμονεῖν, though damaged as indicated, is a new and possibly correct textual variant for the ἁμαρτάνειν of the Bodmer codex. On this and other late copies of Menander, see Eric Handley and André Hurst, *Relire Ménandre* (Geneva 1990) at pp. 143–8, with references to G. Cavallo and H. Maehler, *Greek Bookhands of the Early Byzantine Period, AD 300–800* (1987), where the Bodmer codex is no. 5b and the Cairo codex no. 16b.

10   A sketch for a reconstruction of **9** above. Note that p. 143 is a *left*-hand page: that is to say that the numbering began on the first inside page of the complete codex, a practice that is otherwise known in the ancient and medieval world; but in **6** the odd number 79 is that of a right-hand page, as normally nowadays.

Very few illustrations have survived among the papyri from Antiquity; this irresistible example, from Oxyrhynchus, is a happy exception. It was found in company with documents of the third century AD, and should be contemporary with them.

The scene looks like an act in a circus. Top left are the legs, in boots, of a man swinging through the air as on a trapeze, apparently towards a wreath or padded hoop to the right, while a bear rears up towards him from below; at the right edge, possibly a banner or hanging. Traces of letters appear at top left; but it is not clear what text was associated with the picture; nor is it obvious how the sheet came to be folded vertically and sewn; stitches can be seen along the line of two of the folds, some 35 mm apart.

London, British Library, Pap. inv. 3053: *The Oxyrhynchus Papyri* XXVII (1962) no. 2470 (E. G. Turner), pl. XII. [Colour photograph by EWH for EGT.]

On early book illustrations, see K. Weitzmann, *Illustrations in Roll and Codex* (2nd edn, 1972), and *Late Antique and Early Christian Book Illumination* (1977; with fine colour plates); Turner, *GMAW* under no. 80, pp. 136–7, with more references.

6 *Byzantium*
and the revival of learning
PAT EASTERLING

ꙍ	α
ц	β
ϒ	γ
ꙋ	δ
ϭ	ε
ӡ	ζ
ҏ	η
ϴ	θ
ι	ι
�	κ
⅃	λ
μ	μ
ρ	ν
ӡ	ξ
o	o
ϖ	π
ρ	ρ
σ	σ
τ	τ
υ	υ
φ	φ
χ	χ
ψ	ψ
∞	ω

All Greek books produced in Antiquity were copied in capital script, without word-division and usually without accents or breathings. These, like punctuation, were treated as aids to the reader and not as a fixed part of the text, and they were often added at a stage later than the initial copying. The essence of writing in capitals is that the letters are made individually and are more or less uniform in size, but all kinds of variations could be played on this principle, and scribes often looked for decorative variety, e.g. by widening some letters and narrowing others, or by using contrasting thick and thin strokes.

Capital script in a variety of styles continued to be used for book texts until well into the Byzantine period, but some time late in the eighth century a major change took place, and scribes began using minuscule letter-forms instead of capitals. They saw the advantages of developing a type of script that took up less space and could be written more rapidly, and they used as their models various 'cursive' styles developed over the centuries for less formal purposes than book production, such as the writing of private letters and documents. These types of script used ligatures (strokes linking separate letters together), which made regular 'joined-up writing' possible. As with modern handwriting, there was a danger that the end-product would be hard to decipher; what was needed for book texts was a carefully formalised style. The minuscule script that eventually established itself as the standard achieved this formalism by following strict rules for the shaping and linking of letters. It also made regular use of accents and breathings, which helped readers with word-division (fig. **1** shows the minuscule alphabet, and fig. **3** illustrates a typical ninth-century hand).

Capitals were now kept for special purposes, such as setting off titles or headings, or for marginal commentaries (fig. **4**). What they were *not* used for was to mark proper names, as in modern Greek or English, though much enlarged and sometimes decorated initials were often used to start paragraphs or sections (fig. **2**; and see the examples in figs. **8** and **10**).

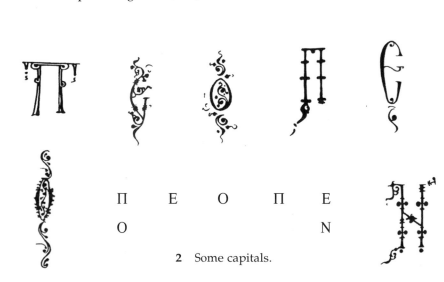

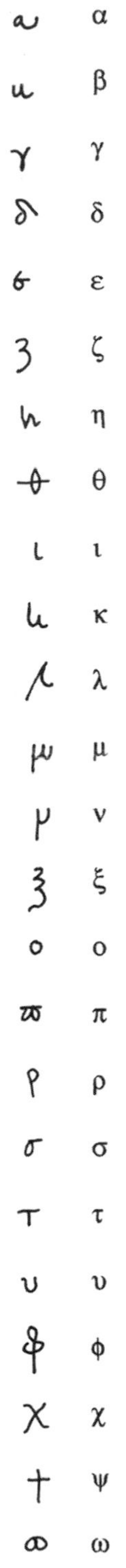

П   Е   О   П   Е

О   N

1 The minuscule alphabet, with its modern equivalent on the right.

2 Some capitals.

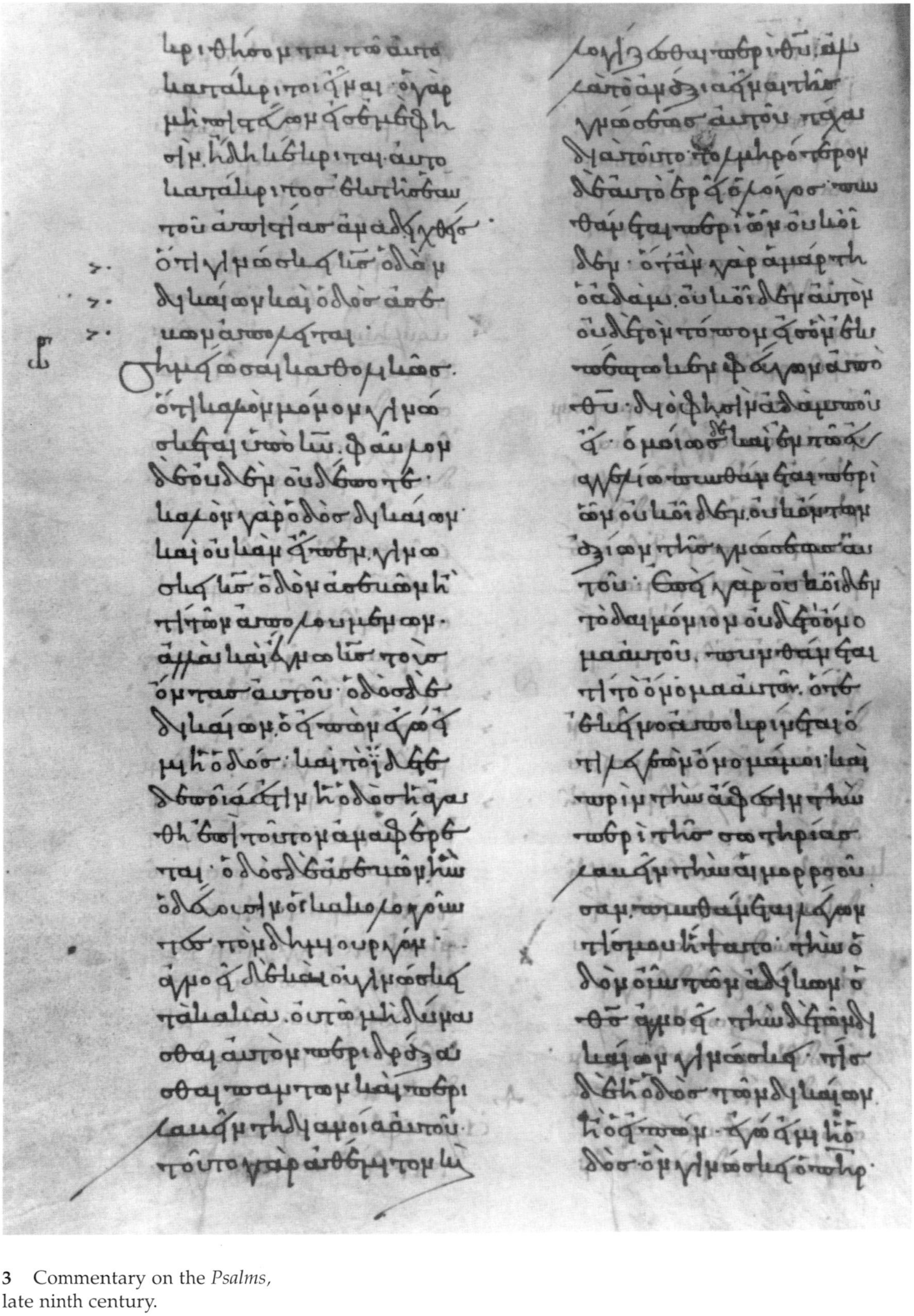

3 Commentary on the *Psalms*,
late ninth century.

4 Sophocles, *Oedipus Tyrannus*, with marginal commentary, tenth century.

Readers became used to minuscule: once they had, they never wanted to go back to the old capital script. This change of fashion must have caused some Classical texts that had survived in libraries for centuries to be thrown out as obsolete, particularly at a time when Christian texts were thought more important and valuable objects of study than pagan ones. The books written in capital script that had the best chance of survival were sacred texts used in church such as Bibles, lectionaries and other kinds of service books, particularly the more luxurious copies, which were treated as objects of veneration. Capital script of a specially ornate kind went on being used for liturgical books long after capitals had stopped being standard for more everyday purposes.

For many centuries the copying of books was largely carried out by monks working in systematically organised monastic scriptoria, the main function of which was to maintain the supply of sacred texts, service books and theological works. But some monastic libraries owned copies of pagan classics too, particularly texts used in school education, like Homer's *Iliad* or a few select tragedies.

'Pure' minuscule writing did not last long: scribes soon started to vary the script by mixing in capital forms and introducing abbreviations of various kinds, some of them shorthand symbols which could have the effect of making the script quite cluttered and difficult to read (fig. **5** gives some examples). In the thirteenth and fourteenth centuries, in particular, there was a trend towards highly idiosyncratic and fanciful styles. But the readers of books were a very small élite in the Byzantine world, and it is not surprising that they developed a taste for arcane and elaborate scripts. Fig. **6** shows how even a clearly written and quite helpfully laid-out text may presuppose sophisticated reading skills.

By the end of the fourteenth century a new market began to open up in Italy, as wealthy humanists looked for a chance to learn ancient Greek and read Greek texts—the New Testament, Homer, the dramatists, Plato, Aristotle, the ancient historians and so on. Scribes writing for readers whose first language was not Greek needed to make their scripts easier to follow; there are many examples from the fifteenth century onwards of more carefully spaced-out texts with fewer ligatures and abbreviations (fig. **7**). By this time there was a steady flow of educated Greeks who were travelling to the West in pursuit of patronage and opportunities to work as copyists and teachers, or sometimes as translators or diplomats. In due course there was scope, too, to work for printers in preparing Greek texts for the press; at all times it was a great advantage to have access to Classical texts not widely available, or to technical treatises in such subjects as mathematics or medicine, astronomy or canon law which were in demand among scholars and professionals of the Renaissance. When the Byzantine empire fell to the Turks in 1453, books as well as copyists had already been moving west for a good half-century.

The people who commissioned, owned or copied the books that have survived have often left traces: sometimes a scribe signs a text and gives a few circumstantial details about himself, the date or place of writing, and the person who paid for the copying (figs **8** and **9**). From scattered bits of evidence we can build up a picture of the activities of some of the most famous monastic scriptoria, but in general we know more about those fifteenth- and sixteenth-century scribes who went to Western Europe, partly because more manuscripts survive from the later period, partly because individuals working independently for patrons were more likely to identify themselves as a form of advertisement.

5 Some common abbreviations:

αν	∠
εν	∠
ας	⌣
αι	⟨
ες	⟩
οις	⌐
αις	⟩⟩
ην	⌒
ιν	⌒˙
ειν	//
ης	ϛ
ις	ϛ̈
εις	ϛϛ
ον	＼
τὸν	⟩
ος	° (above the line)
ου	˘ (above the line)
ουν	ϱ
ους	ϥ
ων	⌒
ως	⌐
ὡς	⌐

54

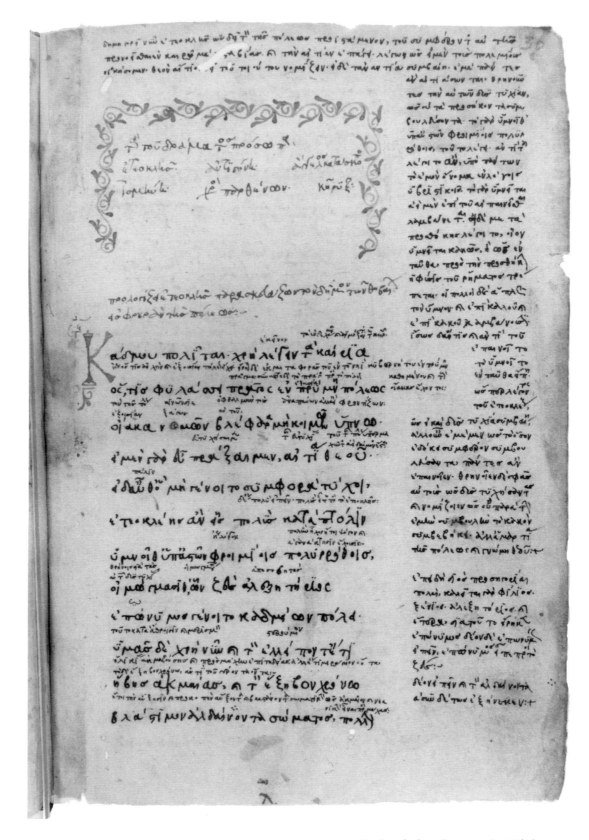

6 Aeschylus, *Seven against Thebes*, with interlinear glosses and marginal commentary, early fourteenth century.

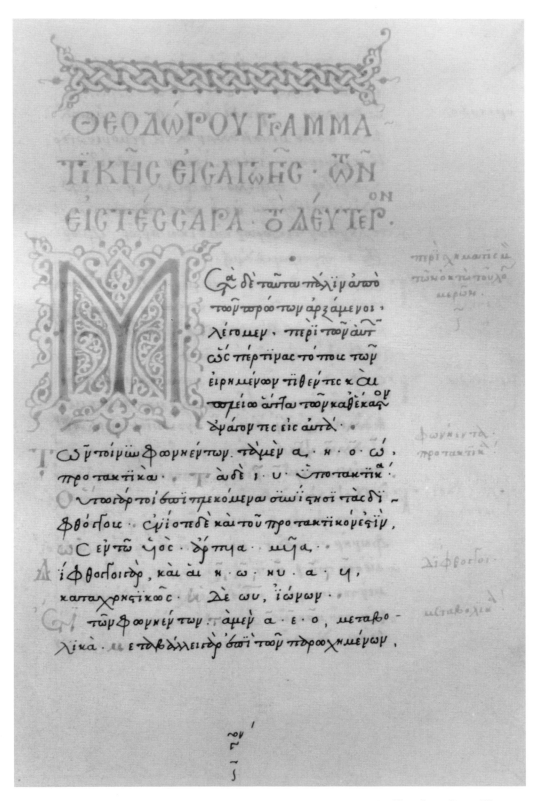

7 Theodore Gaza, *Eisagoge*, copied by *Ioannes Rhosos*, 1479 (?1476).

8 Canons of the Council of Carthage, 1040.

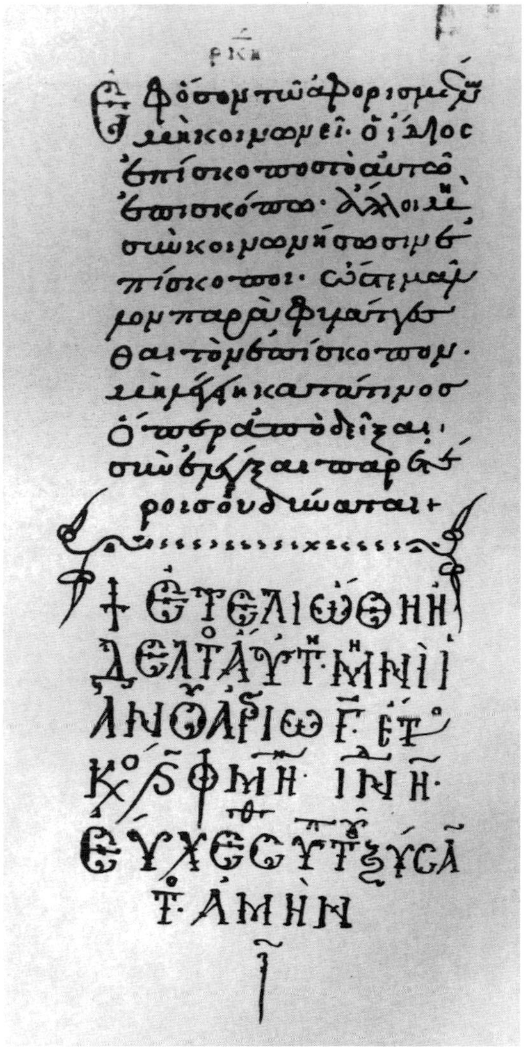

9 Gospels, made in the late fifteenth century for the French scholar G. Budé by the Greek scribe and teacher George Hermonymos.

Hermonymos' subscription is illustrated here.

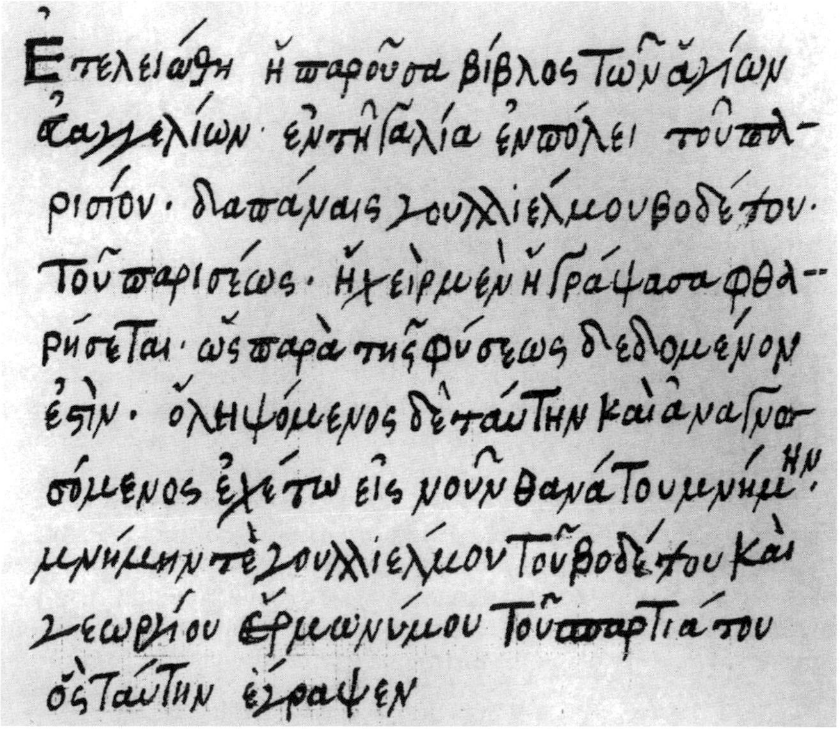

10 Acts and Epistles, thirteenth century (reduced).

Not surprisingly, many of the books that have survived to be preserved over the centuries are fine copies on superior materials (fig. **10**); cheaper and more heavily used books rarely lasted long enough to find their way into modern libraries, but we do have some survivors, to give an impression of what more 'normal' student text-books looked like (fig. **11**); and surviving palimpsests show us how Byzantine scriptoria economised by recycling parchment. Palimpsests (the word means 're-scraped') are books re-made from previously used sheets that have had their original writing (more or less effectively) removed. In some cases the first text remains fairly legible (as in fig. **12**, an eighth-century Gospel book re-used in the thirteenth century) though often it can only be read, if at all, by ultra-violet lamp, or a process of selective image-intensification.

Papyrus had gradually become less easily available for ordinary use during the Byzantine period, and parchment was never cheap; it was a great step forward when paper (made from rags, not wood-pulp) became available as an alternative. From the thirteenth century onwards it was regularly used for book-production, particularly when Italian manufacturers started exporting paper to the Eastern Mediterranean. One useful by-product of this trade from the point of view of palaeographers is that it provided independent evidence for dating: Greek manuscripts are often hard to date on the basis of script alone, but paper, unlike papyrus or parchment, could carry its own identifying (and ever-changing) watermarks, and scholars have been able to establish a chronology from dated documents on watermarked paper.

11 Euripides, *Phoenissae*, with a variety of notes, fifteenth century.

A large proportion of the Greek manuscripts that have survived are safely housed in libraries, catalogued and known to scholars, but new finds are still occasionally made in out-of-the-way monasteries or when minor private collections find their way to the market. Sometimes old texts turn up on stray parchment leaves from discarded books, which were often used to strengthen the bindings of new ones. Since the latter part of the nineteenth century the process of collecting, recording and analysing the evidence has been enormously helped by photography, allowing scholars to compare and identify scripts in books scattered across the libraries of the world. Nowadays, access through the Internet to digitised images of manuscripts opens up an even wider range of new possibilities.

12 The 'Codex Zacynthius', a palimpsest:
Gospels with marginal commentary, eighth-ninth century (lower script);
Gospel lectionary, thirteenth century (upper script)
(reduced: see frontispiece).

SOME FURTHER READING

R. Barbour, *Greek Literary Hands: AD 400–1600* (Oxford 1981)

G. Cavallo and H. Maehler, *Greek Bookhands of the Early Byzantine Period, AD 300–800* (London 1987)

L.D. Reynolds and N. G. Wilson, *Scribes and Scholars* (3rd edn, Oxford 1991)

N. G. Wilson, *Medieval Greek Bookhands* (Cambridge, Mass. 1972)

1   The minuscule alphabet as used in the earliest examples of the script. Capital forms soon began to be substituted for some letters that could easily be confused with others, like *eta* and *kappa*. New minuscule forms later found their way into the alphabet, such as the type of *nu* (ν) used in modern typography.

2   Samples of decorated initials, clockwise: *omicron, pi, epsilon, omicron, pi, epsilon, nu.*

3   Oxford, Bodleian Library, Barocci 235, late ninth century. Part of a page showing a so-called 'catena', or commentary, on the *Psalms*. The script is pure minuscule, and the text is arranged in two columns, as often in manuscripts of this date, no doubt in imitation of the layout of the ancient roll. The three symbols in the left-hand column are quotation marks. The text uses abbreviations for 'sacred names' as in Ch. 5, fig. 6: for example, in the last line of the right-hand column the word 'Father' appears as π̅η̅ρ with a superscript bar.

4   Florence, Bibl. Laurenziana, 32.9, tenth century. This is the most famous of the surviving manuscripts of Sophocles (L). The same volume contains texts of Aeschylus and Apollonius Rhodius; it was acquired for the Florentine humanist Niccolò Niccoli by Giovanni Aurispa in Constantinople in 1422 or 1423. This page shows *Oedipus Tyrannus* 950–97 with the text in minuscules and the marginal commentary in a (mainly) capital script using abbreviations. These small sloping capitals are the descendants of the scholarly handwriting found in notes and corrections to texts from the Roman period onwards, so that they can claim an ancestry of 900 years or more. The page is reproduced here from the facsimile published by R. C. Jebb and E. M. Thompson (London 1885).

5   Some common abbreviations. The habit of abbreviating words by substituting symbols, normally written above or below the line, for familiar endings of the definite article, nouns, adjectives and verbs encouraged a growing tendency to treat the line of text rather freely: letters too could be written above the line, sometimes to save space, sometimes for decorative effects (examples in fig. 6).

6   Cambridge, University Library, Nn. 3.17, early fourteenth century. This shows the opening page of Aeschylus' *Seven against Thebes*, one of the plays studied as part of the Byzantine curriculum. The list of *dramatis personae* is presented within a decorative border, and the lines of text are widely spaced to allow for interlinear glosses and short notes. The marginal commentary is written in a slightly more abbreviated script than the main text, but that too uses some abbreviations.

7   Cambridge, University Library, Ii. 4.16. A copy made at Rome, by the Cretan scribe Ioannes Rhosos, of one of the texts most in demand by humanists eager to learn Greek, the *Eisagoge*, or introduction to Greek grammar, by Theodore Gaza, an influential scholar and teacher who had recently been active in Italy. Rhosos dates the book (fol. 159r) to 1479, but the purchaser, the Englishman John Shirwood, gives the date as 1476. The Greek text is clearly set out and well spaced; the black ink looks as fresh as it must have done over five hundred years ago, but the red-ink decorations have faded. This must have been an expensive copy: the material used is fine vellum, not paper.

8   Cambridge, University Library, Add. MS 1879.9. Canons of the Council of Carthage, one of the doctrine-making councils of the Christian Church, held in 418. This is a fragment of what was evidently intended to be a bilingual text (Greek and Latin?), but only the Greek column was ever copied. The specimen shows the last page, illustrating a large initial *epsilon* at the beginning of the last canon (numbered Π̅Κ̅Η̅ =128) and a subscription in the style of decorative display capitals. The scribe has provided a date (1040) but not his name: the text runs ἐ ΤΕ ΛΙѼΘΗ 'Η ΔΕ ΛΤ(OC) "ΑΥΤΗ · ΜΗΝῚ 'ΙΑΝΟΥΑΡΙѠ Γ̅ · ἔΤ(OC) Κ(ΌCΜΟΥ) ς̅Φ̅Μ̅Η̅ · ΙΝΔ(ΙΚΤΙѠΝΟC) Η̅ · ἔΥΧΕ CΘ(Ε) ΥΠ(Ε P) ΤΟΫ̅ Ξ̅ΫCΑ(Ν)Τ(OC) · 'ΑΜῊΝ ('This text was completed on 3 January in the year of the World 6548, in the 8th year of the indiction.

Pray for the scribe. Amen.') Dates in Byzantine manuscripts are given according to a system which calculates time from the date of Creation, 5508 BC. Numerous examples, ranging from AD 800 to 1593, are given by R. Devreesse, *Introduction à l' étude des manuscrits grecs* (Paris 1952) 286–320. There is a full table of dates in V. Gardthausen, *Griechische Palaeographie* (Leipzig 1913) 488–97.

9   Cambridge, University Library, Ll. 2.13. A luxury copy of the four Gospels, on very fine vellum with gilded and illuminated initials, made in the late fifteenth century for the French scholar Guillaume Budé by the Greek scribe and teacher George Hermonymos, from Mistra in the Peloponnese, who made his career in the West after the fall of Constantinople. In Paris he seems to have had a range of influential pupils, but he was never as significant a figure as Theodore Gaza (fig. **7**). His hand is well suited for reading by non-native speakers of Greek. Hermonymos subscribes the manuscript as follows: Ἐτελειώθη ἡ παροῦσα βίβλος τῶν ἁγίων εὐαγγελίων· ἐν τῇ γαλία ἐν πόλει τοῦ παρισίου· δαπάναις γουλλιέλμου βοδέτου τοῦ παρισέως· ἡ χεὶρ μὲν ἡ γράψασα φθαρήσεται· ὡς παρὰ τῆς φύσεως δεδομένον ἐστὶν· ὁ ληψόμενος δὲ ταύτην καὶ ἀναγνωσόμενος ἐχέτω εἰς νοῦν θανάτου μνήμην, μνήμην τὲ γουλλιέλμου τοῦ βοδέτου καὶ γεωργίου ἑρμωνύμου τοῦ σπαρτιάτου ὃς ταύτην ἔγραψεν ('The present book of the holy Gospels was completed in France in the city of Paris at the expense of Guillaume Budé, the Parisian [Hermonymos twice misspells Budé's name in Greek, and he or someone else has crossed out the intrusive *tau*.] The hand that has done the writing will perish, as is given by nature; but let the person who will take up this book and read it have in mind the remembrance of death and the remembrance of Guillaume Budé and Georgios Hermonymos the Spartiate, who wrote it.')

10 Cambridge, University Library, Add. MS 6678. A fine copy of Acts and Epistles, made in the first half of the thirteenth century. The title (on fol. 44^v), in gold display capitals, shows how decoratively two contrasting scripts could be used. The portrait of St James, at the beginning of his epistle, shows him wearing the classical dress of an apostle with his bishop's scarf as Bishop of Jerusalem.

11 Cambridge, University Library, Mm. 1.11. A working textbook from the fourteenth century: Euripides, *Phoenissae*, with interlinear and marginal notes.

12 Cambridge, Bible Society, MS 213 ('CODEX ZACYNTHIUS'). A palimpsest volume of which the lower writing is a text of the Gospels with commentary (a catena of passages from patristic authorities): the illustration shows part of St Luke's Gospel in a rounded capital script of the eighth-ninth century with marginal commentary (here from St Cyril) in a smaller and narrower hand. The upper writing, at right angles to the original text, is thirteenth-century minuscule. The text is part of a Gospel lectionary, with vermilion rubrication for the notation used to guide the chanting of lessons. The scribe identifies himself with a prayer at the bottom of the page as 'the hapless Neilos').

13 Athos, Vatopedi 328, fol. 131v. In the left-hand column the final words of John Chrysostom's 9th Homily on Paul's *Epistle to the Hebrews* are arranged in the shape of a cross. On the right, the opening of the 10th Homily is enclosed by a decorative border in the shape of a capital Π resting on two ornate columns. The manuscript is a luxury copy of the fourteenth century, on parchment with many elegant decorations, particularly for initial letters and titles. From an illustration (no.17) in Vol. 4 of *Oi Thesauroi tou Agiou Orous*, ed. by P.K. Christou, Ch. Mauropoulou-Tsioume, S.N. Kadas and Ai. Kalamartze-Katsarou (Athens 1991).

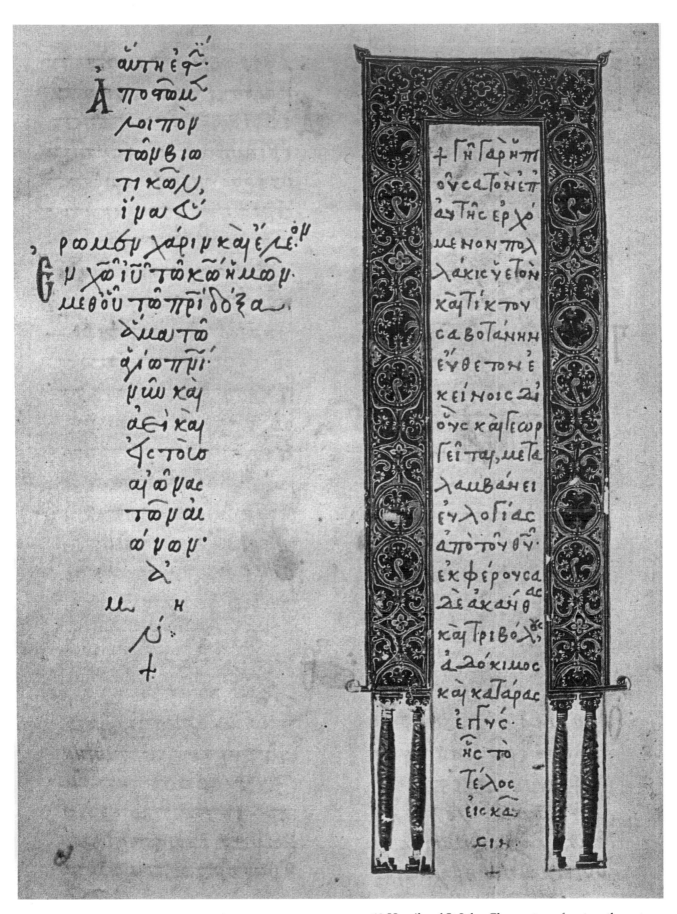

13 Homily of St John Chrysostom, fourteenth century.

7 *From script to print*

E. J. KENNEY

Though isolated experiments in printing with movable types are attested in China and Korea from the eleventh century onwards, typographic printing proper is an independent European invention. The new art spread rapidly from its beginnings around 1450 in Germany and the Low Countries (generally associated with the name of Johannes Gutenberg) to Italy, the home of the New Learning; and by the 1470s editions of classical texts were issuing in quantity from the presses of Venice and Rome and other important cultural centres. The standards of beauty and legibility set by the roman types of early printers such as Nicolas Jenson (*ca.* 1420–80) have never been surpassed. For their models they went back, via the current humanist bookhand, to manuscripts of the ninth century; and this example was followed by the producers of the earliest complete Greek founts. Again it was Jenson who set the standard; and his type of 1471 paved the way for the splendid fount used by the Spanish printer Arnaldo Guillen de Brocar for the Greek Testament in the great polyglot Bible printed at Alcalá in 1514–17 (issued 1522), the Complutensian Polyglot (fig. **1**). This was modelled on a Vatican MS lent by Leo X and said to be 'incredibly ancient'. As always, accents and breathings were clearly a problem. It is one to which there is no really satisfactory solution, short of omission, as was done, for instance, by Politian in his *Miscellanea* (1489) and later by that notorious troublemaker Gilbert Wakefield (1756–1801), who was, in Porson's words, as violent against Greek accents as against the Trinity.

1 Part of a column from the Complutensian Polyglot Bible.

An initial letter from the *editio Brubachiana* of Pindar (Frankfurt 1542).

πᾶσ συρακούσασ. καὶ οἱ τε ἀθηναῖοι ἅμα ἕω ὑπέβαινον, ἐσ τὸ κατὰ τὸ ὀλύμπιϊον, ὡσ
στρατόπεδον καταληφόμενοι. ἦ οἱ ἱππεῖσ οἱ συρακουσίων, πρῶτοι προσελάσαντεσ ἐσ
τὴν καταλύω. καὶ αἰσθόμενοι ὅτι τὸ στράτευμα ἅπαν αὐτῆκται, ἀποστρέψαντεσ ἀγ-
γέλλουσι τοῖς πεζοῖς. καὶ ξύμπαντες ἤδη ἀποτρεπόμενοι, ἐβοήθουν ἐπὶ τὴν πόλιν. ἐν
τούτῳ δ' οἱ ἀθηναῖοι μακρᾶσ οὔσησ τῆσ ὁδοῦ αὐτοῖς, καθ' ἡσυχίαν καθῖσαν τὸ στράτευμα ἐσ χωρίον ἐπιτήδειον. καὶ ἐν ᾧ μάχην τε ἄρξειν ἔμελλον ὁπότε βούλοιντο,
καὶ οἱ ἱππεῖσ τῶν συρακουσίων, ἥκιστ' ἄν αὐτοὺσ, καὶ ἐν τῷ ὄργῳ, καὶ πρὸ αὐτοῦ
λυπήσειν. τῇ μὲν γὰρ, τειχία τε καὶ οἰκίαι εἶργον. καὶ δένδρα, καὶ λίμνη. παρὰ δὲ
τὸ, κρημνοί. καὶ τὰ ἐγγὺσ δένδρα κόψαντεσ, καὶ καπενεγκόντεσ ἐπὶ τὴν θάλασσαν,
παρά τε τὰς ναῦσ, σταύρωμα ἔπηξαν. καὶ ἐπὶ τῷ δάσκωι, ἔρυμά τι ᾗ εὐέφοδώ-
τατον ἦν τοῖς πολεμίοις, λίθοισ λογάδην καὶ ξύλοισ διαχέωσ ὤρθωσαν. καὶ τὴν
τοῦ ἀνάπλου γέφυραν ἔλυσαν. παρασκευαζομένων δὲ, ἐκ μὲν τῆσ πόλεωσ, οὐθεὶσ ἐ
ξιὼν ἐκώλυε. πρῶτοι δὲ οἱ ἱππεῖσ τῶν συρακουσίων προσεβοήθησαν. ἔπειτα δὲ ὕσε
ρον καὶ τὸ πεζὸν ἅπαν ξυνελέγη. καὶ προσῆλθον μὲν ἐγγὺσ τοῦ στρατεύματοσ τῶν
ἀθηναίων τὸ πρῶτον. ἔπει τα δὲ, ὡσ οὐκ ἄν τι προῄεσαν αὐτοῖς, ἀναχωρήσαντεσ καὶ
διαβάντεσ τὴν ἑλωρίδην ὁδὸν, ηὐλίζοντο. τῇ δ' ὑστεραίᾳ, οἱ ἀθηναῖοι ἦ οἱ ξύμμαχοι πα
ρεσκευάζοντο ὡσ ἐσ μάχην. καὶ ξυνετάξαντο ὧδε. δεξιὸν μὲν κέρασ ἀργεῖοι εἶχον ἦ
μαντινέασ. ἀθηναῖοι δὲ τὸ μέσον. τὸ δὲ ἄλλο, οἱ ξύμμαχοι οἱ ἄλλοι. ἦ τὸ μὲν ἥμισυ αὐ
τοῖς τοῦ στρατεύματος ἐν τῷ πρόσθεν ἦν τεταγμένον, τὸ ὀκτώ. τὸ δ' ἥμισυ ἐπὶ ταῖς
εὐναῖσ ἐν πλαισίῳ ἐπὶ ὀκτώ καὶ τοῦτο τεταγμένον. διὸ εἴρητο ᾗ ἄν τοῦ στρατεύμα
τόσ τι ποιῇ, μάλιστα ἐφορῶντας, παραγίγνεσθαι. καὶ τοὺς σκευοφόρουσ ἐντὸς τού-
των τῶν ἐπιτάκτων ἐποιήσαντο. οἱ δὲ συρακύσιοι, ἔταξαν τοὺς μὲν ὁπλίτασ, ἐφ' ἑκ
καὶ δέκα ὄντασ πανδημεὶ συρακουσίουσ, καὶ ὅσοι ξύμμαχοι παρῆσαν. ἐβοήθησαν δὲ
αὐτοῖς σελινούντιοι μὲν μάλιστα. ἔπειτα δὲ καὶ γελῴων ἱππεῖς, τὸ ξύμπαν ἐσ δια
κοσίουσ. καὶ καμαριναίων ἱππεῖς, ὅσον εἴκοσι. καὶ τοξόται, ὡς πεντήκοντα. τοὺς δὲ
ἱππέασ ἐπετάξαντο ἐπὶ τῷ δεξιῷ. οὐκ ἐλάσσον ὄντασ, ἢ διακοσίουσ καὶ χιλίασ. πρὸσ
δ' αὐτοὺς καὶ τοὺς ἀκοντιστάσ. μέλλουσι δὲ τοῖσ ἀθηναίοισ προτέροισ ἐπιχειρήσειν, ὁ νι
κίασ, κατά τε ἔθνη ἐπιπαριὼν ἕκαστα, καὶ ξύμπασι τοιάδε παρεκελεύετο.

ΔΗΜΗΓΟΡΙΑ ΝΙΚΙΟΥ.

» Πολλῇ μὲν παραινέσει ὦ ἄνδρεσ τί δεῖ χρῆσθαι. οἳ πάρεσμεν ἐπὶ τὸν αὐτὸν ἀγῶ-
» να. αὐτὴ γὰρ ἡ παρασκευὴ ἱκανωτέρα μοι δοκεῖ εἶναι θάρσος παρασχεῖν, ἢ καλῶς
» λεχθέντες λόγοι, μετὰ ἀσθενοῦσ στρατοπέδου. ὅπου γὰρ ἀργεῖοι, καὶ μαντινέασ, καὶ
» ἀθηναῖοι, καὶ νησιωτῶν οἱ πρῶτοι ἐσμεν, πῶσ οὐ χρὴ μετὰ τοιῶνδε καὶ τοσῶνδε ξυμ
» μάχων πάντα, τινὰ μεγάλην τὴν ἐλπίδα τῆσ νίκησ ἔχειν; ἄλλως τε καὶ πρὸσ αὐ
» δρασ πανδημεὶ τε ἀμυνομένουσ, καὶ οὐκ ἀπολέκτουσ ὥσπερ καὶ ἡμᾶσ. καὶ προσέ
» τι σικελιώτασ. οἳ ὑπερφρονοῦσι μὲν ἡμᾶσ, ὑπομενοῦσι δὲ, οὔ. διὰ τὸ τὴν ἐπιστήμην τῆσ
» τόλμησ ἥσσω ἔχειν. παραστήτω δέ τινι καὶ τόδε, πολύ τε ἀπὸ τῆσ ἡμετέρασ αὐτῶν
» εἶναι. καὶ πρὸς γῇ οὐδεμιᾷ φιλίᾳ, ἥντινα μὴ αὐτοὶ μαχόμενοι κτήσεσθε. καὶ τοὐ
» ναντίον, ὑπομιμνήσκω ἡμᾶσ, ἢ οἱ πολέμιοι σφίσιν αὐτοῖς εὖ οἶδ' ὅτι παρακελεύ-
» ονται. οἱ μὲν γὰρ, ὅτι περὶ πατρίδος ἔσται ὁ ἀγών. ἐγὼ δὲ, ὅτι οὐκ ἐν πατρίδι ἐξ ἧς κρα
» τεῖν δεῖ, ἢ μὴ ῥᾳδίως ἀποχωρεῖν. οἱ γὰρ ἱππεῖς πολλοὶ ἐπικείσονται. τῆσ τε οὖν ὑμε
» τέρασ αὐτῶν ἀξίασ μνησθέντεσ, ἐπέλθετε τοῖσ ἐναντίοις προθύμωσ. καὶ τὴν πα
» ροῦσαν ἀνάγκην καὶ ἀπορίαν φοβερωτέραν ἡγησάμενοι τῶν πολεμίων.

Ὁ μὲν νικίασ, τοιαῦτα παρακελευσάμενος, ἐπῆγε τὸ στρατόπεδον εὐθύσ. οἱ δὲ
συρακούσιοι ἀπροσδόκητοι μὲν ἐν τῷ καιρῷ τούτῳ ἦσαν, ὡσ ἤδη μαχούμενοι. καί τι
νὸσ αὐτοῖς ἐγγὺσ, τῆσ πόλεωσ οὔσησ καὶ ἀπεληλυθέτων. οἱ δὲ καὶ διὰ σπουδῆσ προσ
βοηθοῦντεσ δρόμῳ, ὑστέριζον μὲν, ὡσ δὲ ἕκαστόσ πη τοῖσ πλείοσι προσμίξειε καθί
σταντο. οὐ γὰρ δὴ προθυμίᾳ ἐλιπεῖσ ἦσαν, οὐ δὲ τόλμῃ, οὔτ' ἐν ταύτῃ τῇ μάχῃ, οὔτ' ἐν
ταῖς ἄλλαισ. ἀλλὰ τῇ μὲν ἀνδρείᾳ, οὐχ ἥσσον ἐσ ὅσον ἐπὶ τὴν ἐπιστήμην ἀντεῖχον. τῷ δὲ ἐλλεί
ποντι αὐτῆς, καὶ τὴν βούλησιν ἄκοντες προὐδίδοσαν. ὅμως δὲ οὐκ ἂν οἰόμενοι σφὰσ
σι τοὺς ἀθηναίους προτέρουσ ἐπελθεῖν. καὶ διαταχέισ ἀναγκαζόμενοι ἀμύνασθαι
ἀναλαβόντεσ τὰ ὅπλα εὐθὺσ ἀντεπῄεσαν. καὶ πρῶτον μὲν αὐτῶν ἑκατέρων, οἵ τε
λιθοβόλοι, καὶ σφενδονῆται, καὶ τοξόται, προὐμάχοντο καὶ τροπὰσ οἵασ εἰκὸσ ψι

Λ L iii

2 Thucydides
(Aldus, Venice 1542).
The *editio princeps*.

Unfortunately Greek typography, instead of following the relatively simple evolutionary course of the roman letter, had meanwhile taken a wrong turning.

The trend-setter was Aldus (Aldo Manuzio, 1449–1515), who elected to adopt the rival fashion of basing types on the contemporary Greek bookhand. In order to cope with the contractions and ligatures, some hundreds of different type-forms were required; and the many practical disadvantages were not redeemed in this case by the beauty of the result (fig. **2**).

The artistic possibilities of the approach were indeed splendidly realised in the famous French Royal types, the 'Grecs du Roi', cut by Claude Garamond (*ca.* 1480–1561) after the handwriting of the Cretan calligrapher Angelo Vergecio (fig. **3**). A fount numbering some 400 sorts is obviously both unpractical and uneconomic, but simplification was very slow to evolve.

3   Justin Martyr (R. Stephanus, Paris 1551).

στρώμνή, δικαίων τ' ὀμμάτων παρουσία.

εἰ δ' ἄλλο πρᾶξαι δεῖ τι βουλιώτερον,   660

ἀνδρῶν τόδ' ἔστιν ἔργον, οἷς κοινώσομεν.

ΟΡ. ξένος μέν εἰμι Δαυλιεὺς ἐκ Φωκέων·

στείχοντα δ' αὐτόφορτον οἰκείᾳ σάγῃ

ἐς Ἄργος, ὥσπερ δεῦρ' ἀπεζύγην πόδας,

ἀγνὼς πρὸς ἀγνῶτ' εἶπε συμβαλὼν ἀνήρ,   665

ἐξιστορήσας καὶ σαφηνίσας ὁδόν,

Στρόφιος ὁ Φωκεύς, πεύθομαι γὰρ ἐν λόγῳ—

Ἐπείπερ ἄλλως, ὦ ξέν', εἰς Ἄργος κίεις,

πρὸς τοὺς τεκόντας, πανδίκως μεμνημένος,

τεθνεῶτ' Ὀρέστην εἰπέ, μηδαμῶς λάθῃ·   670

εἴτ' οὖν κομίζειν δόξα νικήσει φίλων,

εἴτ' οὖν μέτοικον, εἰς τὸ πᾶν ἀεὶ ξένον,

θάπτειν, ἐφετμὰς τάσδε πόρθμευσον πάλιν·

νῦν γὰρ λέβητος χαλκέου πλευρώματα

σποδὸν κέκευθεν ἀνδρὸς εὖ κεκλαυμένου.—   675

τοσαῦτ' ἀκούσας εἶπον. εἰ δὲ τυγχάνω

στρωμνή: vid. Porson. ad Eurip. Or. 1051. Vel legi possit στρω-μναί. Vid. Musgrav. ad Eurip. Suppl. 1120.

660. βαλιώτερον Ald.

663. στείχων δι' αὐτόφορτον Rob. αὐτόφυρτοι οἰκίαις ἄγῃ Ald.

664. οὖπερ P. Bigot. ἀπεζύγαν

Ald.

668. ἄλλος Ald.

670. μὴ δαμῶς Ald.

675. κεκαυμένου Aurat. Stanl. Abresch. Sed vulgatum recte tu-etur Butlerus, monens εὖ κεκλαυ-μένου respicere ad inferias juste ac pie persolutas.

4   Aeschylus, *Prometheus Vinctus*, ed. C.J. Blomfield (Cambridge 1810).

The decisive break with the cursive tradition was signalled in 1741 by the Homer issued at Glasgow by the Foulis brothers; it was not, however, until 1810 that a fully satisfactory modern type emerged in the shape of 'Great Porson Greek', cut as its name implies under the supervision of Richard Porson (1759–1808), him-self an exquisite calligrapher (fig. 4). Though finally purged of all contractions and ligatures, it betrays its calligraphic ancestry by its slope and the shape of cer-tain letters, notably the *gamma*, features which still persist in its descendants, familiar from the Oxford Classical Texts and the Loeb Classical Library.

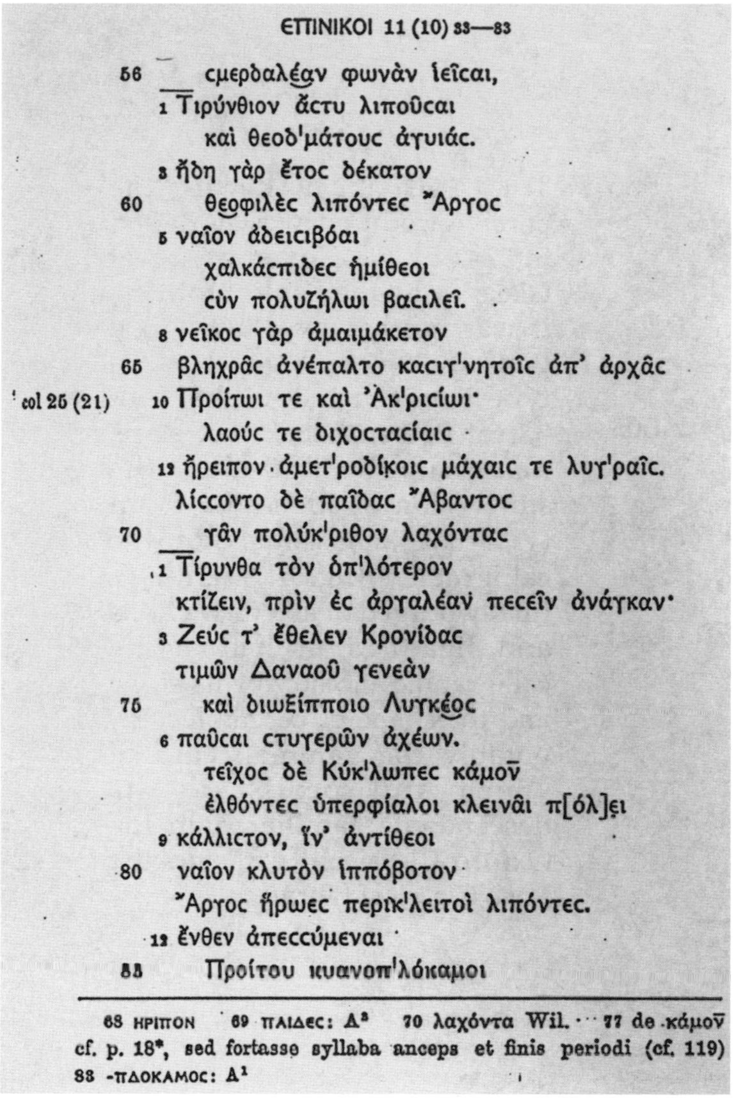

<pre>
   56 ‾ cμερδαλέαν φωνὰν ἱεῖcαι,
      1 Τιρύνθιον ἄcτυ λιποῦcαι
         καὶ θεοδ'μάτουc ἀγυιάc.
      3 ἤδη γὰρ ἔτοc δέκατον
   60   θεοφιλὲc λιπόντεc Ἄργοc
      5 ναῖον ἀδεισιβόαι
         χαλκάcπιδεc ἡμίθεοι
         cὺν πολυζήλωι βαcιλεῖ.
      8 νεῖκοc γὰρ ἀμαιμάκετον
   65   βληχρᾶc ἀνέπαλτο καcιγ'νήτοιc ἀπ' ἀρχᾶc
   col 25 (21) 10 Προίτωι τε καὶ Ἀκ'ρισίωι·
         λαούc τε διχοcταcίαιc ·
      12 ἤρειπον· ἀμετ'ροδίκοιc μάχαιc τε λυγ'ραῖc.
         λίccοντο δὲ παῖδαc Ἄβαντοc
   70   γᾶν πολύκ'ριθον λαχόνταc
      1 Τίρυνθα τὸν ὁπ'λότερον
         κτίζειν, πρὶν ἐc ἀργαλέαν πεcεῖν ἀνάγκαν·
      3 Ζεύc τ' ἔθελεν Κρονίδαc
         τιμῶν Δαναοῦ γενεὰν
   75   καὶ διωξίπποιο Λυγκέοc
      6 παῦcαι cτυγερῶν ἀχέων.
         τεῖχοc δὲ Κύκ'λωπεc κάμον
         ἐλθόντεc ὑπερφίαλοι κλεινᾶι π[όλ]ει
      9 κάλλιcτον, ἵν' ἀντίθεοι
   80   ναῖον κλυτὸν ἱππόβοτον·
         Ἄργοc ἥρωεc περικ'λειτοὶ λιπόντεc.
      11 ἔνθεν ἀπεccύμεναι ·
   83   Προίτου κυανοπ'λόκαμοι
</pre>

---

68 ΗΡΙΠΟΝ   69 ΠΛΙΔΕC: A²   70 λαχόντα Wil. ·· 77 de ·κάμον
cf. p. 18*, sed fortasse syllaba anceps et finis periodi (cf. 119)
83 -ΠΛΟΚΑΜΟC: A¹

5 Bacchylides, ed. B. Snell
(Leipzig 1934).

More recently there has been a welcome and long overdue return to the older and purer models. The pleasing modification of M.E. Pinder's 'Griechische Antiqua' used by Teubner in some of their editions (fig. **5**) represents a lost opportunity, having been regrettably abandoned in favour of the 'dull and lumpish' fount (Victor Scholderer's words) that is still the uniform of the series. Of more lasting influence has been the trend set by Robert Proctor with his magnificent 'Otter' types (fig. **6**), which hark back to the Complutensian Polyglot. That did not prove suitable for commercial exploitation; a more successful initiative in the same vein is Victor Scholderer's 'New Hellenic', based on a Venetian fount of 1492. This is familiar in books published by the Cambridge University Press, which has adopted it as its standard Greek type-face (fig. **7**).

ΟΔΥΣΣΕΙΑΣ ΒΙΒΛΟΣ ΠΡΩΤΗ. ΘΕΩΝ
ΑΓΟΡΑ. ΑΘΗΝΑΣ ΠΑΡΑΙΝΕΣΙΣ ΠΡΟΣ
ΤΗΛΕΜΑΧΟΝ.

Ἄνδρα μοι ἔννεπε, Μοῦσα, πολύτροπον, ὃς μάλα πολλὰ
πλάγχθη, ἐπεὶ Τροίης ἱερὸν πτολίεθρον ἔπερσε·
πολλῶν δ' ἀνθρώπων ἴδεν ἄστεα καὶ νόον ἔγνω,
πολλὰ δ' ὅ γ' ἐν πόντῳ πάθεν ἄλγεα ὃν κατὰ θυμόν,
ἀρνύμενος ἥν τε ψυχὴν καὶ νόστον ἑταίρων.
ἀλλ' οὐδ' ὣς ἑτάρους ἐρρύσατο, ἱέμενός περ·
αὐτῶν γὰρ σφετέρῃσιν ἀτασθαλίῃσιν ὄλοντο,
νήπιοι, οἳ κατὰ βοῦς Ὑπερίονος Ἠελίοιο
ἤσθιον· αὐτὰρ ὁ τοῖσιν ἀφείλετο νόστιμον ἦμαρ.
τῶν ἁμόθεν γε, θεά, θύγατερ Διός, εἰπὲ καὶ ἡμῖν.

  Ἔνθ' ἄλλοι μὲν πάντες, ὅσοι φύγον αἰπὺν ὄλεθρον,
οἴκοι ἔσαν, πόλεμόν τε πεφευγότες ἠδὲ θάλασσαν·
τὸν δ' οἶον, νόστου κεχρημένον ἠδὲ γυναικός,
νύμφη πότνι' ἔρυκε Καλυψώ, δῖα θεάων,
ἐν σπέσσι γλαφυροῖσι, λιλαιομένη πόσιν εἶναι.
ἀλλ' ὅτε δὴ ἔτος ἦλθε περιπλομένων ἐνιαυτῶν,
τῷ οἱ ἐπεκλώσαντο θεοὶ οἶκόνδε νέεσθαι
εἰς Ἰθάκην, οὐδ' ἔνθα πεφυγμένος ἦεν ἀέθλων,
καὶ μετὰ οἷσι φίλοισι. θεοὶ δ' ἐλέαιρον ἅπαντες
νόσφι Ποσειδάωνος· ὁ δ' ἀσπερχὲς μενέαινεν
ἀντιθέῳ Ὀδυσῆϊ πάρος ἣν γαῖαν ἱκέσθαι.

  Ἀλλ' ὁ μὲν Αἰθίοπας μετεκίαθε τηλόθ' ἐόντας,
Αἰθίοπας, τοὶ διχθὰ δεδαίαται, ἔσχατοι ἀνδρῶν,
οἱ μὲν δυσομένου Ὑπερίονος, οἱ δ' ἀνιόντος,

β

6   Homer, *Odyssey* (printed at the
University Press, Oxford 1909).

ΘΕΟΚΡΙΤΟΥ ΕΠΙΓΡΑΜΜΑΤΑ

I

Τὰ ῥόδα τὰ δροσόεντα καὶ ἁ κατάπυκνος ἐκείνα
ἕρπυλλος κεῖται ταῖς ʿΕλικωνιάσιν·
ταὶ δὲ μελάμφυλλοι δάφναι τίν, Πύθιε Παιάν,
Δελφὶς ἐπεὶ πέτρα τοῦτό τοι ἀγλάισεν·
5 βωμὸν δ᾽ αἱμάξει κεραὸς τράγος οὗτος ὁ μαλός
τερμίνθου τρώγων ἔσχατον ἀκρεμόνα.

I (A.P. 6. 336)   1 ἁ Anth.   ἡ cett.   2 ἕρπυλλος Anth. D² Cal. -υλος KCD
4 ἐπεὶ Iunt.Cal.   ἐπὶ cett. | πέτραι Anth. | τοι Anth. D² in ras. Iunt.Cal.   οἱ K
5 ὁ μᾶλος Anth.   ὁμαλός C Iunt.Cal.   ὁ μανός KD

7   Theocritus, ed. A.S.F.
Gow (Cambridge 1950).

α β γ δ ε ζ
η θ ι κ λ μ
ν ξ ο π ρ σ
τ υ φ χ ψ ω

Kadmos™,
a computer-based fount, as
used in this publication.

SOME FURTHER READING

For a comprehensive survey, see Konstantinos Sp. Staikos, *Charta of Greek Printing. The Contribution of Greek Editors, Printers and Publishers to the Renaissance in Italy and the West* (Cologne 1998)

Nicholas Barker, *Aldus Manutius and the Development of Greek Script and Type in the Fifteenth Century* (2nd edn, New York 1992)

J.H. Bowman, 'Robert Proctor's "Otter" Greek type', *Transactions of the Cambridge Bibliographical Society* 9 (1989) 381–98

W.H. Ingram, 'The ligatures of early printed Greek', *Greek, Roman & Byzantine Studies* 7 (1966) 371–89

E.J. Kenney, *The Classical Text* (Sather Classical Lectures XLIV, Berkeley, California 1974)

M.S. Macrakis, *Greek Letters from Tablets to Pixels* (New Castle, Delaware 1996)

R. Proctor, *The Printing of Greek in the XVth Century* (Oxford 1900, repr. Hildesheim 1960)

V. Scholderer, *Greek Printing Types 1465–1927* (London 1927)

NOTES ON THE CONTRIBUTORS

PAT EASTERLING, co-editor and contributor, is a fellow of Newnham College, Cambridge, and has been Regius Professor of Greek (1994–2001); from 1987 to 1994 she was Professor of Greek at University College London. She works on Greek literature, with a special interest in the transmission and reception of tragedy. At present she is preparing a commentary on Sophocles' *Oedipus at Colonus*.

CAROL HANDLEY, co-editor, has been a Senior Member of Wolfson College since 1989. She is a former Head of Camden School for Girls (1971–1985), and a past President of the Classical Association (1996–7). Her special interests are in the teaching of Greek language and Literature to beginners and to mature students, and she has for some years been organising weekend courses in Greek for Cambridge University's Board of Continuing Education at Madingley Hall.

ERIC HANDLEY, contributor and design consultant, is a Fellow of Trinity College, Cambridge, and Professor of Ancient Literature at the Royal Academy of Arts. He was Regius Professor of Greek at Cambridge, 1984–94, and before that Professor of Greek at University College London and Director of the Institute of Classical Studies. His main interests are in Greek Drama and ancient Theatre Production, especially in Comedy, and especially in new texts recovered from papyri.

E.J. KENNEY is Emeritus Professor of Latin in the University of Cambridge and an Emeritus Fellow of Peterhouse. He has published editions of works by Lucretius, Ovid and Apuleius, and has explored some aspects of the history of the printing and editing of classical texts in *The Classical Text* (1974; Italian translation by Aldo Lunelli, *Testo e metodo*, 1995). He is at present working on a commentary on Ovid, *Metamorphoses VII-IX* for the Fondazione Lorenzo Valla.

JOHN KILLEN is Emeritus Professor of Mycenaean Greek at Cambridge and a Fellow of the British Academy. Having graduated in Classics from Trinity College Dublin in 1959, he became a research student at Cambridge under the direction of John Chadwick, who collaborated with Michael Ventris in the decipherment of Linear B. He has remained at Cambridge ever since, becoming a Fellow of Churchill College in 1961 and of Jesus College in 1969. He specialises in the epigraphy and interpretation of Linear B, and has a particular interest in Mycenaean economy and administration. He is joint author with J.-P. Olivier of the standard edition of the Knossos tablets in transcription and with John Chadwick and others of the recently completed four-volume Corpus of Mycenaean Inscriptions from Knossos (Cambridge/Rome).

HAROLD B. MATTINGLY was Professor of Ancient History at the University of Leeds from 1970 to 1987. He then retired to Cambridge, where he continues research and writing. His main interests are fifth-century BC Greece and Rome in the Hellenistic World.

JOYCE REYNOLDS is Emerita Reader in Roman Historical Epigraphy and Honorary Fellow of Newnham College, Cambridge, and Somerville College, Oxford. She collects and comments on Greek and Latin inscriptions, especially in Cyrenaica and Turkey.

T.R. VOLK is an Affiliated Lecturer in the Faculty of Classics, Cambridge, where he lectures on Coinage. As well as teaching at Cambridge (since 1976/7), he has held visiting positions at the Universities of Vienna, Rome (Tor Vergata) and Saragossa, and has curated exhibitions both at home and abroad. His publications include studies of ancient coin-circulation and the history of numismatics.

ACKNOWLEDGEMENTS

THIS BOOK could not have been put together without the kind collaboration of a number of libraries, learned institutions, publishers and others to whom the editors and contributors are indebted for illustrations and permission to reproduce them here. In particular we should like to thank the The Archive of the Libyan Department of Antiquities, Shahat, Cyrenaica, the Bible Society, the Biblioteca Medicea Laurenziana Florence, the Bodleian Library Oxford, the British Museum, Cambridge University Library, Cambridge Classical Faculty Library and Museum of Classical Archaeology, C. Dobias-Lalou, Deutsches Archäologisches Institut Athen, the Egypt Exploration Society, the Fitzwilliam Museum Cambridge, the Institut de Papyrologie, Paris, the Institute of Classical Studies, Liverpool University Archaeological Museum, Gbr Mann Verlag, the Monastery of Vatopedi, Mount Athos, New York University (Aphrodisias Excavation), Princeton University Press, the Society for the Promotion of Roman Studies, Trinity College Cambridge and University College London.

Many friends and colleagues have given generous help and advice; we are especially grateful to Jeannie Cohen, John Easterling, Charlotte Roueché, Richard Hunter, Bert Smith and Sara Owen. The whole volume has benefited enormously from the exemplary skill and patience of Nigel Cassidy, the Cambridge Classical Faculty's photographer.